SMALL-RIVER FLY FISHING
FOR TROUT AND GRAYLING

Welsh Terrier

Stokesay

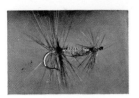

Border Mayfly

Barrett's
Professor

Blue Variant

Amorous
Shrimp

Barrett's
Bane

Kite's
Imperial

Brown Squirrel
Nymph

Welsh Fusilier

Abergavenny

Quill Polo Nymph

BORDER FLIES

JAMES EVANS

Small-River Fly Fishing
for Trout and Grayling

ADAM & CHARLES BLACK
LONDON

FIRST PUBLISHED 1972
REPRINTED 1977
BY A. AND C. BLACK LIMITED
35 BEDFORD ROW, LONDON WC1R 4JH

ISBN 0 7136 1228 2

This Book is Dedicated to
the Members, past, present and future of
THE GAMEFISHERS' CLUB
whose headquarters are in Birmingham,
as an inadequate expression of my gratitude for the
many, many happy hours I have spent fishing on their
waters, where so many lessons have been learned.

Printed Offset Litho in Great Britain by
Cox & Wyman Ltd
London, Fakenham and Reading

CONTENTS

FOREWORD

A NEW book by a new author, the immediate reaction of most fishermen is to shrug their shoulders and accept it as one of the harsher facts of life, or should they be presented with a copy at Yuletide by a well-meaning relative or friend, it will no doubt be relegated to the bookshelf to join the host of other indifferent volumes on our favourite sport that have been published this century. However, occasionally we see the publication of a new book that is way above the average, either because the author has exceptional talent in the literary sense or a unique knowledge on the chosen subject. This new book *Small-River Fly Fishing* by James Evans falls in the latter category.

I have been connected with James Evans in business for many years, and I am also privileged to look upon him as a friend. A keen fly fisherman for most of his life, he has resided in the Midlands for many years, and during this period has spent much of his leisure hours fishing on rough border streams mainly in Wales. He has consequently built up a very sound and extensive knowledge on this rather specialised type of fishing. I use the word specialised here very much with my tongue in my cheek, as while we fly fishermen residing in the South of England probably look upon small river fishing as specialised, it is probably far from the truth. I do not doubt that overall there are more fly fishermen engaged fishing on such waters than there are fish in the more glamorous chalk streams. This outlook has probably been fostered by the lack of books on small river fishing, whereas there have been literally hundreds of books written about our chalk streams.

I feel sure that Jim, as he is known to his many friends, has written a classic that will be looked upon as a leading guide for this type of fishing for many years to come. In business he is extremely meticulous and pays great attention to detail, consequently I am absolutely certain that the many theories and observations he makes in his new book should be treated with considerable respect.

JOHN GODDARD

Chapter One

TERMS OF REFERENCE

It is almost a convention among authors of books on trout fishing to begin by pointing out that possibly more books have been written on this subject than on any other participant sport; they usually then go on to give their opinions on why this should be and round it off by giving their own reasons for adding one more to the list.

Let me say here and now that my own reason for writing this book is because I want to; if additional excuse is needed, let it be that my own sector of the subject is one which has received rather less literary attention than some of the others.

I don't honestly know why there should be such a relatively large number of books on trout fishing: it could have something to do with the fact that we have to struggle through the longest close season in the angling calendar, and are thus left with plenty of time for reading and writing; that is, of course, those of us who for reasons of non-availability or personal choice do not go after the grayling on an equal footing to the trout, which in my view it most certainly deserves—especially in the type of waters that this book is about.

Alternatively, perhaps it is because trout fishermen in general tend to come from the more articulate and possibly the more literate section of the community. Publishers after all are not conspicuously more benevolent than other men, so that one can only assume the existence of a demand sufficient for them to deem it worthwhile to supply; certainly many trout fishermen of my acquaintance are the most avid readers of everything on the subject that they can lay their hands on.

Commendable as this thirst for knowledge may at first sight

appear to be, it nevertheless bothers me: let me try to explain why.

If one examines critically the majority of books on river trout fishing, from the earliest classics right down to the present day, one soon realises that most of them are written by fortunate men whose main—often exclusive—experience of the sport has been confined to the chalk-streams of the south of England.

It is hardly necessary nowadays to point out that for every fisherman who has access to chalk streams there are literally hundreds who have to make do with something different: yet it is a fact that books and even articles in angling magazines have an overwhelming preponderance on the side of the chalk streams; I do not know why this should be; perhaps it is an extension of the reason given above for the proliferation of trout fishing books in general.

Nor must we stop at the segregation of chalk streams and " the rest ": for " the rest " is also subdivided, although the distances between the many subdivisions are not generally so great.

It follows that the man who reads every book he can find on river trout fishing (I deliberately exclude those on the stillwater side of the sport, since their titles usually distinguish them clearly), must read a very high proportion of those concerned with chalk streams: I am thinking in particular of those men who are in the earlier stages of their enslavement by the sport, and who will be less selective and more un-critical in their reading; these must, often unknowingly, absorb large doses of indoctrination which, while quite valid for the type of fishing enjoyed by the author of the particular book or article, are nevertheless completely inimical to that pursued by the reader. I know—it happened to me.

To the angler with experience of both types of river the differences between them are obvious, as are the conclusions to be drawn from those differences; not so the unfortunate tyro who comes in at the point where a river is simply water moving between two banks.

Apart from the fundamentals such as rod, line and artificial fly, from the trout fisherman's point of view the chalk stream differs, often radically, from what we might call a rain-fed stream at almost every point of comparison. Let us examine a fairly typical chalk stream.

Except after long periods of excessive weather conditions such as droughts and unusually wet seasons, the level remains fairly constant at the " full " position; this is because our chalk stream is relatively independent of day-to-day weather changes, drawing most of its water in a steady flow from the vast " sponges " of chalk in which it has its sources: except under the influence of a local cloud-burst its water is usually of unbelievable clarity.

This clarity is often further enhanced by a very even surface flow which can look deceptively slow until an artificial fly is dropped on it: the careful observer can see every spot on a feeding fish, and not merely its rise-form; conversely, of course, the fish has at least an equally good view of the angler!

The absence of turbulence which gives rise to this apparent surface placidity is due to an even and often almost level bottom of even depth, an even width and almost vertical sides.

Almost continuous along the bottom are vast beds of dense sub-aqueous weed, each large enough to hide a shoal of outsize fish; later in the season this weed will emerge above the surface and become a nuisance unless cut.

In general the banks of most chalk streams are fairly open and uncluttered by an excess of bushes and trees: this of course means that most of the time a long conventional overhead cast can be used without too much danger of either the forward or back cast getting into trouble; the angler is able to remain far enough away from his fish to avoid scaring it, which is just as well in view of the clarity of the water.

Apart from the snails and crustacea in which every chalk stream abounds—shrimps, crayfish, etc.—the principal diet of the fish will be the various members of the insect order *Ephemeroptera* in either their nymph, dun or spinner stages; the appearance of these, usually in very great abundance, will often be as predictable and regular as clockwork, as will be the reaction of the fish to them: the main complication which can arise out of this is when stages of more than one insect are occurring at the same time; olives might be hatching at the same time as iron blues, or caenis may be hatching among a fall of blue-winged olive spinners: under such conditions selective feeding may be encountered—that is the fish will be taking one species and ignoring the other.

Various sedges and some of the small stone flies also occur on chalk streams, usually concentrated in sufficient quantity to constitute a " hatch " and to engender a general " rise ".

The chalk stream fisherman therefore, may act in one of two ways: he can quietly walk his water looking for a feeding fish (either rising regularly or darting about after nymphs), and then fish for it in the appropriate manner; alternatively he can settle himself comfortably in a suitable position and simply wait for the rise (or fall, should it be of spinners); when it happens he will identify the fly on which the fish are feeding, select the appropriate artificial, and commence to fish.

This then is a description of a fairly typical chalk stream and its fishing: I confess to over-simplification and doubtless many who have more experience of chalk streams than I will be able to put forward countless exceptions to what I have said; nevertheless it is a fair general picture.

Chalk stream fish, because of that same abundance of food which enables them to be selective, have a faster growth rate and greater optimum size than those in other waters, newly flooded reservoirs excepted.

Now let us look at a " rain-fed " stream.

By definition it is subject to the vagaries of the weather: heavy rain followed by dry spells make it go up and down like a Yo-yo; the rain does not need to occur in the locality in which one is fishing, for a cloudburst in the hills among which the stream has its source can later in the day bring up the level dramatically as one watches; however, if the rain is local it can have an immediate effect on the colour and the clarity of the water, which can persist to a degree for days and even weeks afterwards, as countless ditches continue to leach their soil-laden drainage into the main stream.

After continuous heavy rain it will come into spate and be bank high and the colour of cocoa, and often take considerable time to settle down to a normal flow; after weeks of drought it will become so thin and clear that one wonders where the fish that one knows to be there can find to hide themselves.

Open stretches of bank on the smaller rain-fed rivers—or the higher reaches of larger ones—are normally few and far between, most are well bushed to a greater or lesser degree, and a few are almost impossibly so from the point of view of the fly-fisher: this is probably because the land through which they flow, being less rich, is not so intensively cultivated as that along the chalk streams and the big rivers of the plains; also a healthy binding of tree roots is essential to the banks to lessen the effect of scouring during spates.

Casting is therefore rarely as described in most of the text books: the side cast is probably the one most frequently employed, together with flicks, switches and all manner of extemporary expedients to which formal names have never been given.

In width our rain-fed stream can vary from broad, shallow rippling stickles to narrow, deep pools—often very deep indeed where overhanging tree roots have been undercut; the unevenness of the bottom engendered by these variations is often increased by the presence of large stones or even boulders. The effect of all this is a surface in constant movement in all directions varying from gentle rippling to downright turbulence; only in broad pools or long slow glides is anything approaching a smooth surface encountered.

The presence of a fish is usually only recognised by the appearance of a rise form on the water; fish are rarely seen in the water except in conditions of unusual clarity when the light and the observer's position are just right; unless, of course, the fish are leaving hurriedly!

The larder available to the fish in a rain-fed stream is far from being as comprehensive or as super-abundant as that at the disposal of his chalk stream cousin; the size of the former is in consequence proportionately very much less, though size-for-size his fighting qualities must earn him every respect. Except on exceptional and possibly carefully preserved waters a three-quarter pound trout is noteworthy, a pounder exceptional and anything over that something to boast about for the rest of the season. Where they are encountered the grayling tend to be larger—often much larger—than the trout, although not often seen by purely trout fishermen not actually looking for them.

The diet of fish in such streams is catholic in the extreme, and most of it is obtained off the bottom: washed-in worms and grubs, aquatic nymphs and larvae, drowned terrestrial insects, berries in season, shrimps, snails and crayfish if they are fortunate enough to live in a stream containing them; small fish of their own and other species, and also the eggs of their own and other species are all fair game. On the comparatively rare occasions when they are tempted to come up and feed off the surface it will often prove to be on terrestrial insects which have got there inadvertently; every sort of land-based fly gets onto the water at some time, and most are acceptable to the trout and grayling in a rain-fed stream. I once caught a trout of above average size for the water which was stuffed to the gills with wasps. Small caterpillars of the variety which lower themselves on threads, and who have misjudged the length of their threads, are always prized, as are the ones which just tumble in, and also spiders.

Specific species of insects which interest the rain-fed fish are primarily the smaller kinds of stone fly (and the large ones in some rivers, particularly in the north country where they are known as mayflies), various sedges, and, in my experience a very poor third (excepting the true mayfly, where it occurs), various up-winged flies of the *Ephemeroptera*.

The number of times on which I have encountered a general and sustained rise to a specific insect on a rain-fed stream I could count on the fingers of my two hands. I have only once seen a truly selective rise (to the sherry spinner) during which the fish would look at nothing but the specific natural insect.

It follows from the foregoing that it is the exception rather than the rule for a fisherman on a rain-fed stream to be able to cast to a regularly rising fish: he will often cast to where he has seen a fish rise (not the same thing at all); or he may cast to where he thinks there may be a fish and "bring it up". (This is an occurrence, fortunately very common on our sort of water, which I have discovered is quite beyond the comprehension of friends whose only experience is of chalk streams.) He may also fish the likely spots with an upstream nymph, or on wider streams fish the water generally with downstream wet flies.

I hope that I have been successful enough in highlighting the many differences between the two types of fishing to show that the rain-fed river angler who has been nurtured on a diet of chalk stream literature is likely to find himself at a grave disadvantage; such, indeed, was my own experience as a newcomer to fly fishing. I recall particularly my frustration at never being able to keep my fly afloat as a result of my strict adherence to the injunction: "hackle very lightly—not more than two turns"; this on waters where today I appreciate that as many as ten turns are not necessarily excessive.

This brings me to the point that I am trying to make. Namely that authors of books on fishing, particularly river fishing for trout, in addition to—or perhaps even instead of—commenting on the number of such books already in and out of print, should state clearly and unequivocally their own Terms of Reference regarding the type of fishing to be investigated. Even more important they should make absolutely clear the type of water to which they will be referring.

Before moving on I feel that special reference should be made to magazine articles: many of these I find to be particular offenders in their failure to be specific about the type of water concerned; often this may be put down to lack of space; what the writer wants to say may need 1,500 words and the editor may only have room for 1,200; so pruning is necessary, either by the author himself or by a sub-editor; so things get left out, among them the few words specifying the type of water. Here I am taking the charitable view, though it cannot always be like that, and I suspect that the reason may more frequently be lack of thoughtfulness.

When an angler reads a book or an article about his sport, the picture painted by the author superimposes itself upon the picture already in the angler's own mind of his own favourite water; he relates one to the other subconsciously if not consciously. Unless he is given clear notice at the outset of his reading that this is not something that he can exactly relate to his own activities, he is going to absorb information which can put him on the wrong foot for possibly a long time.

True, given such notice at the outset our angler may well decide not to read the book or piece at all: I cannot think, however, that many angling authors would resent this, or even knowingly feed a fellow angler with ideas which might detract from the enjoyment or success of his personal fishing.

Now, therefore, let me put myself in order by stating my own Terms of Reference as far as this book is concerned.

My title is taken from the preamble to the prospectus of the Gamefishers' Club, an extremely friendly, enthusiastic and democratic society (in spite of a rather pretentious title), most of whose members live in and around Birmingham, who do me the honour of having me as their president.

The full text is as follows:

" The Club offers about $6\frac{1}{2}$ miles of small-river fly-fishing for brown and rainbow trout and grayling on streams in Worcestershire and on the Welsh Border in Herefordshire, Radnorshire and Shropshire . . ."

The streams referred to are the Leigh Brook (a tributary of the River Teme), the Rivers Redlake and Lugg, and the Hindwell Brook (a tributary of the Lugg). Add to these my own experience of the Clun, Teme, Onny, Monnow, Usk, Dove, Teifi, the upper Severn and the upper Wye and others of similar type, and you have a fair cross-section of the sort of water I am describing. Since most of these are in the vicinity of the Welsh Border I shall refer to them from now on, in the interest of brevity, as " Border streams "; their counterparts can be found in profusion all over the British Isles with the exception of the south and east of England. I realise that to a large number of people, especially in North Britain, " Border " must imply the Scottish border, and I trust that they will not resent my use of the term in my own context : after all, nearly everything I have to say about my Border refers to theirs also.

In addition to the characteristics I have already described I would define a Border stream as one which at normal level can safely be waded across at reasonably frequent points : its banks in general are high, so that with the exception of gravel spits on the insides of the bends it is often necessary to get down into or alongside the water in order to fish.

I wish that I could say that this is a book for beginners. This cannot be because I realise that I am not gifted enough to write for true beginners; very few of us are, because in the process of acquiring the necessary knowledge and experience to justify the writing of a book at all, one forgets just what it is like to be a complete beginner. I set out to write as simply as possible and to avoid any " blinding with science ", but I am already conscious of having used terms and jargon which will be incomprehensible to a beginner. It must also be very easy to omit facts which seem too trivial to mention, but which nevertheless may be vital links in the so-far incomplete chain of a beginner's understanding.

This is not to say that a beginner will not learn anything from this book; I very much hope that he may : but as with all learning he will need to read it in conjunction with other writings : he will also need to look elsewhere for more detailed information about such things as knots, line-splicing, casting, fly-dressing and artificial flies in general, and entomology : all these things and more

I shall touch on, but only to scratch the surface in the context of what I am trying to say in general; to do these subjects justice would require several books, each specialised, and of course such books already exist, written by more knowledgeable people than I. The titles of some of the best of these (on many of which I have drawn for this book) will be found from time to time in footnotes at appropriate places.

Finally let me assure my reader, assuming that he has got this far, that if his main interest is in the direction of chalk stream, big river or still-water fishing for trout or grayling, or fishing for salmon or sea trout, or spinning or bottom fishing for trout or grayling, or for that matter coarse fishing or sea fishing, then this is not the book for him.

POLLUTION AND ABSTRACTION

There is one factor which is common to both chalk streams *and* Border rivers, and indeed to all fishing everywhere, and that is the increasing volume of pollution and its attendant evil, abstraction.

By pollution I do not mean only crude aquatic pollution, but terrestrial and atmospheric pollution also, both of which are equally disastrous to fish by interrupting or unbalancing their food chain. Nor are stillwaters and reservoirs immune from these latter evils.

By abstraction I do not mean only direct abstraction from the rivers by farmers and horticulturists for irrigation, and by water authorities for public consumption; equally damaging but even more insidious are boreholes, possibly miles from the river but in its watershed, sunk by industry and public authority in numbers beyond the credibility of the man in the street, which rob the rivers by sucking away the water table from beneath them.

The level of pollution now existing in rivers, even supposing that it can be contained, is, Heaven knows, much too much; the fact that it is even tolerable is solely due to the diluting effect of the flow of the water in the river: reduce that flow and there is no dilution and your river is well on the way to becoming an open sewer.

Some of those who fish mountain and moorland streams— most of which I include in my generic term of " Border " waters —imagine themselves immune from the twin evils of pollution and abstraction; but they delude themselves. Abstraction down-stream of them will create a faster run-off of their own water, abetted by the drainage department of the river authority, who consider it their duty to get the water into the sea in the shortest possible time. Pollution downstream of them will deprive anglers downstream of their fishing, and in increasing numbers they will start to find their way upstream to compete with our Border fisher-men for their hitherto spacious—and inexpensive—waters.

I sometimes take time off to wonder what sort of fishing will be available to my grandchildren, assuming that they will not be millionaires, and I am thankful that I was not born into a later generation.

Perhaps the most successful organisation in attacking pollution on behalf of the fisherman is the Anglers' Cooperative Associa-tion, which works effectively through the Common Law at a time when the penalties for polluting our rivers under Statute Law are derisory.

The A.C.A. has joined battle impartially with giants of industry and statutory authority, and won impressively; but not without expense. It deserves the full support of every fisherman, not least the man who has come to think that there is little he can do per-sonally to combat a problem that is national and indeed inter-national. But unless each individual angler *is* prepared to use his voice and at the same time contribute a small tithe of what he actually spends on his fishing, he may well find that he has no fishing, within his means, available to him.

Chapter Two

THE TOOLS FOR THE JOB

PERHAPS THIS is as good a point as any to reveal that I have spent a large portion of my working life in the fishing tackle industry; this does not, of course, qualify me in any way to teach others how to fish. I remember well some years ago a rather acrid exchange in the correspondence columns of the angling press concerning salmon fishing methods: one of the protagonists was a well-known angler and angling writer who rashly based the authority of his point of view on the fact that he had spent a lifetime in the fishing tackle industry. " Upon what," he asked, " does Mr. So-and-so base *his* authority?" Mr. So-and-so maintained a dignified silence, but one of his supporters reacted smartly: " Mr. So-and-so," he said in effect, " has certainly not spent his lifetime in the fishing tackle industry; Mr. So-and-so has spent *his* lifetime catching salmon."

However I digress. What my experience of the tackle trade does help me to do is advise on the selection of tackle, particularly in the negative sense. Most anglers buy a great deal more equipment than they need or can ever use, and a lot of their pleasure is derived from the purchasing of new bits of tackle. This also gives pleasure to the trade, which probably could not survive without the additional fillip of impulse buying. In the tackle trade there is a cynical little saying to the effect that while some tackle is made for catching fish, quite a lot more is for catching fishermen. You cannot entirely blame the trade for this, since the fishermen concerned quite obviously want to be caught. Perhaps the best example of this is to be found in floats. Many coarse fishermen cannot pass a tackle shop without buying a float, and in consequence finish up with literally hundreds—every one no doubt excellent for its purpose—

yet they will confine their fishing to half-a-dozen tried but battered patterns.

The best British fishing tackle is the finest in the world. There can be no argument about this. It is probably also the most expensive. There is also a great deal of British tackle which, while falling only a little short of the best in excellence, is considerably cheaper. There is, happily, very little bad British tackle, and such as there is will mostly be found in the coarse fishing sector. In addition there is nowadays a wide selection of imported tackle, and some of this is also very good and often very reasonable in price. Here, however, perhaps more careful discrimination is needed in making a choice. Finally there is the " half-and-half " product—the piece of equipment which is manufactured in this country but whose main components are imported. This usually means that the home produced equivalents are either non-existent or not good enough, and the chief example of this is the fibreglass rod. Rapid strides are being made in the design and manufacture of British hollow glass blanks, and in the near future there is no doubt that these will hold their own against any in the world. But at the moment of writing the majority of fly rods in this material offered to a prospective customer will be made with imported blanks.

RODS

Let us now discuss the requirements of a rod to be used for Border stream fishing.

If you are proposing to fish a team of wet flies across and down on one of the larger rivers such as the Teme or the Usk, then probably the best length of rod is nine feet with a fairly easy action. This can be in three sections, although two are to be preferred. This length enables the flies to be properly controlled and the line to be " mended ". " Mending " the line means converting a downstream belly in it into an upstream one, by means of a flick of the rod, thus allowing the flies to swing down more nearly at the speed of the current.

However, for the more general run of Border fishing, when most of the casting will be upstream, the ideal length of the rod in my view is from seven to eight feet, in two pieces—a " brook " rod, in fact. If it were shorter a great deal of control will be lost, both over the fly on or in the water, and over the hooked fish. If it were longer one is up against the problem of casting in confined spaces, and there are usually more of those than the other sort.

It is a fallacy to suppose that a longer rod will necessarily cast further or more accurately than a shorter one, particularly within the limits of our subject. More important is the " action " of the particular rod, but even that is entirely subordinate to the skill of the caster. A really skilful caster will get his distance and accuracy with almost any rod, or even a broom-stick.

On the relative merits of built split cane and tubular fibreglass I am not going to put myself out on a limb. I shall confine myself to certain facts and observations and thereafter the reader must draw his own conclusion according to his own personal findings.

At this moment in time the best split cane emphatically makes a better fly-fishing rod than the best hollow glass. Whether this verdict will persist with the imminent advent of compound tapers in fibreglass or the more distant prospect of carbon fibre, I cannot say.

However it would be grossly misleading for me were I to suggest that the most expensive rods were desirable for Border fishing. They are not. This is simply because the limitations imposed by the intimate nature of the fishing rarely calls for the extra degree of performance to be found in a really first-class rod.

Further down the cost scale a good deal more parity exists between split cane and glass. Please note that I say " split " cane or " built split-cane " and not just " built-cane ". There is an important distinction. All good cane fly rods are made of *split* cane, which implies that the six segments making up the rod are each riven from the original bamboo by causing it to split along its grain. They are then straightened and shaped to precise limits by highly skilled craftsmen. Machines can assist, but only in a subordinate capacity. Consider how much cheaper it would be if these sections were sawn by machines to the same accuracy, but with the saw crossing and recrossing the grain instead of following it. This is not always to say that a rod which is described as " built-cane " is necessarily sawn built-cane, but certainly with cheaper rods it might be wiser to be sure.

The best split-cane comes from " male Japanese Tonkin " bamboo (mostly from China) of large diameter—about three inches—whose nodes or knots occur at least twenty-four inches apart. Obviously the thinner or younger the original bamboo pole the closer together the nodes. While an eighteen inch interval is acceptable, one should beware of anything substantially less. It is customary for the nodes on the strips of cane used to make up a rod to be staggered for strength purposes, since the node itself is the weakest point in the strip of cane. This is normally done alternately so that three of the nodes occur at a point half-way between the other three. Some craftsman rodbuilders however prefer to stagger the nodes in a spiral, which is probably marginally stronger still.

A rod in which adjacent nodes appear to lie together should not be touched with a barge-pole, as should one with so much decorative whipping that the nodes cannot be seen at all. For this could mean that at best the rod has been put together without regard to the staggering principle, or at worst that it is made up of only two or three strips of cane and then planed to appear to have the six facets of a properly built rod.

In a well-made split-cane rod the glue lines between the strips of cane should be almost invisible: one should be able not so much to see them as to see where they should be! If, therefore, the glue lines are obvious or irregular or have any small gaps, you would be advised to look at another rod.

There is, of course, more to the making of a split-cane rod than the mechanics of building it. Of paramount importance is the curing and " tempering " of the original bamboo. This will not only determine much of the action of the rod—whether it be on the stiff or the soft side—but also on whether in later life (or earlier in some), it will be likely to take a " set ". That is, if it will acquire a permanent bend, either in consequence of prolonged use or an encounter with a particularly intransigent fish. This is something which it is almost impossible to judge of by looking at a new rod, and wherein one's main safeguard is the reputation of the manufacturer or dealer.

Fibreglass, of course, being a man-made material, is subject to none of the vagaries which affect cane. It owes little to the man who makes it but much to the one who designs it. The designer decides on the ideal thickness of wall and degree of taper within the limits of the blanks available to him. Only rarely can the same man design the rod first and then the blanks to suit it. Tubular glass is virtually unbreakable (except in car doors) and cannot take a set. In the bigger rods, for example for conventional reservoir fishing, I find that it casts as far as cane except when cutting into the wind, but is slower than cane in killing a good fish; these factors, however, do not concern us here.

For Border fishing rods, therefore, I find little to choose between split-cane and hollow fibreglass. I possess both types but confess that I use the fibreglass ones most. My reason for this is that in the bushed conditions which I encounter not only in my fishing but also frequently in the approach to the water, the fibreglass is less prone to damage. I must emphasise, however, that this is a factor to which consideration should be given *only* after a reasoned decision has been made purely on the basis of fishing efficiency.

The action of a rod for Border fishing should be simply workmanlike. There is no requirement for fancy tapers which in more expensive rods give a longer cast or more delicate presentation. Delicacy of presentation is just as important here, of course, but at the shorter ranges more depends on the caster than the rod. The action should be strictly medium—not too stiff, nor yet too soft. A description of my own experience may be a useful pointer.

For several years I had fished happily and successfully with a rod which I knew to be too stiff. It was in fact one which I had converted myself from an early Canadian seven-foot hollow glass spinning rod. I had got over the stiffness problem by using a rather heavy floating line, and liked the outfit because it called for a fast casting action which gave the fly (or so I thought) less time to get caught up behind me. Then a friend invited me for a day on his water on a small—much smaller than I was accustomed to—hill stream at a time of very low water. We worked upstream together, taking alternate pools. My friend had an ancient hybrid rod—the butt section was greenheart and the top split-cane—of very easy action. His line was an old silk one, the dressing of whose taper was largely absent. Every time I cast to a fish, no matter how delicately I tried to put down my fly, that fish was away, accompanied by all his friends in the pool. When my friend cast he almost always rose his fish and was able to cast again to other fish in the pool without disturbance.

Horrified by this experience, I immediately swung to the other extreme and acquired an unusually soft-actioned rod, this time in split-cane, which took the lightest obtainable line. Undoubtedly this worked. I found that I was catching more fish in thin water conditions and obviously scaring less. And even if these were smaller ones I was clearly preventing them from going off and scaring better fish further up. The only snag was that the extremely easy action of the rod called for a commensurately easy casting action. Hangups became more frequent and accuracy went haywire, particularly if there was any sort of a breeze from a frontal direction.

Compromise was clearly called for, and was achieved in the rod which I am currently using—seven feet six inches, once more in hollow fibreglass, with a medium action and a silk line whose weight falls in between those of the first two.

And there you have it in a nutshell; a medium-actioned rod—not too stiff, not too soft; and a medium-weight line—not too heavy, not to light—but as fine as possible.

In a rod of the type and length that we are discussing, weight is not an important factor, although obviously it is to be avoided unnecessarily. Lined or " jewelled " butt-and-tip rings are bulky and subject to fracture, with sometimes disastrous effects on line-coating. I find that " hard chrome " butt- and end-rings are far lighter and neater, and are not so prone to grooving.

Many rude things have been written in the past about snake intermediate rings. I have a feeling that like many other inexplicable angling maxims this is something which has become a bit of angling folk-lore as a result of being handed down from generation to generation of angling writers, although the original reason for the stricture has been lost. All I can say is that I find the modern stainless steel snake rings superior to all types both in lightness and in the ease with which the line shoots through them. There is the minimum of friction without any loss of line control.

In recent years a sort of inverted snobbery has reacted against the former rather fussy finish of the quality fly rod. Every unnecessary embellishment has been stripped off and often the more expensive a rod is the more utility it appears. I am only partially in agreement with this, since, along with the old aphorism that there is more to fishing than catching fish, I feel that there may be more to a fishing rod than a mere implement for catching fish. A craftsman-made tool loses nothing by being beautifully finished, and if some modest additional decorative whipping enhances its eye-appeal this will often enhance pride of ownership and pleasure in using. However such things as fly-keepers and most shoulder collars are superfluous without being decorative, as is, of course, close whipping on a glass rod. Nor is this necessary on a good modern split-cane rod, since the adhesives used to bind the strips of cane are stronger than the cane itself and require no support. Contrary to a lot of opinion, however, I am personally satisfied that firm close-whipping will stiffen a split-cane rod if this is needed.

I do have strong views about fly rod handles; those on many cheaper rods are too fat and I am convinced that the grips of most factory-made rods, including the best, are too long, and waste part of the rod. If you hold a fly rod as if you are fishing with it and measure the extent of the grip covered by your hand, including your extended thumb, you must have a very large hand if this comes to much more than six inches; the only way that this length can be exceeded is if the rod is held with the forefinger along the top of the butt, but this grip, although widely practised, is not a very good way of holding the rod; the grips of most production rods are considerably longer than this, and combined with what is usually an excessive space allowed for the reel seating, tend to make the handle as a whole unwieldy.

In my view the reel should lie as close behind the casting hand as possible, and I like to be able to feel my own against my little finger. This has the effect of reducing to the minimum the leverage created by the weight of the reel which can make for fatigue. In many rods which have long grips and the reel fitting near the extreme tip of the butt, the distance between the hand and the reel, and the leverage thereby imposed, are I think excessive.

Another bit of angling folk-lore is that an outfit composed of rod, reel and line should balance at the point of grip, or sometimes at some other nearby " ideal " position, with so many yards of line hanging outside the top ring. This is quite fallacious as far as modern tackle is concerned although it may have had some substance with the weapons of the past. It is still perpetuated to-day, however, and I have actually encountered people seeking to buy heavier reels so that this " balance "—and the exact opposite of what I have postulated above—can be achieved. Indeed it is still possible to purchase specially lead-loaded butt-buttons (in assorted weights) for this purpose.

Obviously a tip heavy outfit is to be avoided as much as a butt-heavy one unless there is to be excessive fatigue. But the only true " balance " in a fly-fishing outfit is that between the power of the rod and the weight of the line (which *is* important, and of which more later), and has nothing to do with a fulcrum.

Still on the subject of butts, I personally favour a screw winch fitting even on a small rod. There is a slight sacrifice of weight but this I find is outweighed by the positiveness and reliability of the attachment of the reel to the rod. Where a screw-fitting is employed it is virtually impossible for the reel to fall off in a moment of crisis. I don't think it is possible to say this of any other arrangement. It is important, however, that the thread of the reel fitting should be *behind* the reel, and not in front of it. The latter, front-end thread, will take the reel away from the hand and towards the butt, whereas a rear thread will bring it closer to the hand.

On my own rods, the butts of which I have made myself, the front end of the screw-winch fitting is " buried " in the corks of the grip back to the edge of the forward reel slot. A further " saddle " of half-round corks is fitted over the next inch-or-so of the winch fitting. It is on this " saddle " that the heel of my hand rests, allowing my little finger to lie against the cage of the reel. I have referred to this cork " saddle " in inverted commas since it is not to be confused with the saddle fitting of the reel itself, which is the attachment to the reel by which it is fixed to the rod. This reel saddle is often unnecessarily long, the manufacturers erring on the side of caution. If it is shortened, by sawing and/or filing, the thread on the reel fitting can also be shortened, often by as much as an inch, making a further useful saving on butt length. By the above means I have been able to contract the over-all butt length of my rod to an entirely adequate 7¼ inches *including* the screw-winch fitting. In fact, even when fitted with a butt-spear, which I habitually use, it is still substantially shorter than the butts of most production rods.

After my fussiness about the length of the butt the attachment to it now of a spear may at first seem something of a paradox. However I do not see it this way because I regard all my efforts to shorten the butt as worthwhile *if only* to allow of the inclusion of a spear. I regard the butt-spear as one of the most useful accessories to fly-fishing and am constantly surprised that so few other anglers use one. So small is the demand for these that they are quite difficult to obtain, certainly the light alloy flat-bladed type which are the only suitable ones. I make use of mine constantly. It enables me to shove my rod-butt safely into the nearest bank, leaving me with both hands free to attend to fly, leader or netted fish. When one is lunching, gossiping or simply sitting looking at the water, it enables the rod to be stored in a safe, upright position instead of lying in the grass at the mercy of passing boots or hooves.

REELS

The coarse fisherman, the sea fisherman, the salmon and sea trout fisherman and the reservoir trout fisherman all use their reels for either assisting them to cast, controlling their tackle or controlling a hooked fish, or for a combination of two or all three of these purposes.

For the Border fly-fisherman the reel is simply a winch for the convenient storage of line. Such gadgets, therefore, as adjustable drags, variable checks and devices to allow finger control of a running fish, are superfluous and so much extra weight, and in some cases hazardous, in that they can provide additional protuberances round which the line or leader may become snagged. The main requirements of a Border fly reel are lightness, reliability (with which I couple simplicity) and reasonably rapid retrieve. This latter characteristic is best achieved by ensuring that the reel has a fairly narrow drum (not more than three-quarters of an inch inside) and an outside drum diameter of not much less than three inches.

Such a drum will hold a lot more line than will be needed for fishing purposes, but in order to take full advantage of the diameter for the purposes of rapid retrieve it will need to be comfortably full. There must therefore be some sort of packing under the line. For reels which may be required to deal with a running fish this packing is achieved by backing. Backing is additional line, monofilament, braided nylon or terylene, or some other cord of reasonable strength, which is spliced to the inside end of the fly line and then wound on the reel underneath the line. The method is in the first instance to wind the fly line direct onto the reel outside end first. The backing is then spliced to the rear end of the fly line, and that also is wound onto the reel until it is comfortably full. The combined line and backing are then taken off the reel, reversed, and put on the right way round. This method is usually employed with a Border reel also, but since backing as such is unnecessary and to save a little weight I line the inside of my drum with cork. There are two ways of doing this; a cork bung such as is used for making rod-handles can be shaped, split and fitted round the drum centre; or a strip of sheet cork of the appropriate width can be wound round the drum until only sufficient room is left for the fly line.

Multiplying fly reels have been around for some time, but until recently have been represented only by extremes; on the one hand a cheap and tinny French one and on the other an expensive and cumbersome product best suited to the reservoirs. However the introduction of a new model more in keeping with my type of fishing—but still expensive—led me to giving it a try on my own waters; the object of course is an extremely rapid rate of retrieve, a most necessary requirement in Border fly fishing as in any other sort. If you require to get line back on your reel quickly in order to cast to a fish which has become apparent much closer to you, or if you hook a fish which proves larger than expected and you are caught with yards of loose line around your feet, or if you simply want to reel in in order to move on, the rapid cranking of a small-diameter single-action reel can be tiresome. This is my reason for specifying earlier a three-inch narrow drum for a single-action reel.

However after a fair trial I must report that I do not favour a multiplier for Border fishing; with the relatively short length of line involved I quickly discovered that the rate of retrieve was *too* fast, and that often before I realised what was happening my fly was in my top ring! That of course is something which could be got over with practice, and is not the main disadvantage: this proved to be a propensity to over-run (ever a bugbear of multiplying reels) as a result of stripping off line preparatory to casting; several feet of line would become loose coils on the reel with the first pull, and if this was not noticed the second and subsequent pulls would so exacerbate the situation as to jam up the reel. All this can be avoided, of course, either by the careful drawing off of each length of line, or by having the check set so hard that over-running could not happen, but both expedients would be self defeating.

Bearing in mind then the additional weight involved and also the fact that a multiplier of its very nature must incorporate an additional amount of rather delicate machinery, thus providing both a potential additional source of trouble and a departure from our initial aim of simplicity, I think that this type of reel is best left alone for our sort of fishing.

One mechanical device which I regard as essential to a fly reel is dual checkwork, the effect of which is to make the reel usable either left- or right-handed: the check on a fly reel should exert a rather greater resistance when the line is being pulled off than when it is being replaced; one reason for this is to avoid over-runs when the reel is rotated sharply, as happens when the line is being stripped off during casting, and also in tightening, when this is done " off the reel "; it also helps in controlling a good fish when one is encountered, provided one is first able to get all one's loose line back on the reel. Similar strength of resistance is not required when retrieving line, since it makes the job of reeling in more fatiguing and also creates unnecessary noise. Some reels are arranged so that the check-pawl gives a similar resistance both ways, but most allow for a variation as described above. Since these would reverse themselves if a right-handed reel were used left-handed, alternative sets of check-work should be included, so that one pawl can be turned out of action and the other engaged.

For some reason I have never been able satisfactorily to resolve, the majority of game fishermen—at any rate of my acquaintance— being right-handed, use their reels right-handed: I have yet to be successful in persuading any of them to try it the other way, and yet it has always seemed to me logical for a right-handed man to fish more efficiently by winding his reel left-handed: not to do so means that having cast, before putting any line back on his reel he must change over his rod from his right hand to his left; and then back again before he can make another cast; in the meanwhile, should he hook a fish, he must control—or even play—it with his left hand, while his dexter hand has only the mechanical job of cranking the reel. The majority of coarse fishermen are not affected by this prejudice, be they users of centre-pin or fixed-spool reels, although it could be argued that reel control is more important to them than to fly-fishermen. It is noticeable that many of the fly-fishermen who do use their reels left-handed have come to this branch of the sport *via* coarse fishing; perhaps there is an element of snobbery in right-handedness!

Conventional fly reels are of the " cage-drum " type, and it would be difficult to improve on this general design. The cage consists of a fixed protective rim within which the outside of the drum

—that is the handle side—revolves: this rim is attached to the back-plate of the reel on the opposite side of the drum at four points—call them North, East, South and West when the reel is looked at from the handle side; North is at the junction of the reel and its saddle, and East, South and West consist of struts, with West being the strut on the edge of the reel facing the rod-rings; in some reels these struts are short lengths of circular-section rod into which the back-plate and protective rim are screwed or riveted : however in better fly reels the back-plate and cage are an all-in-one casting.

I have gone into some detail in describing the cage-drum reel because it leads me to a hobby horse of my own regarding fly reels which I shall now expound : in fairness I should say that I have yet to encounter anyone who has emulated me in this; nevertheless I am personally happy at the soundness of the idea.

The line comes away from the underside of the reel in a forward direction; in the case of a simple cage-drum reel this would be between the West and the South struts : some reels have a line-guide ring, either metal or even " jewelled ", situated alongside or in place of the West strut. Now probably the most violent movement in casting is when the line is being stripped off the reel; but when this is done the line is pulled backwards almost parallel to the axis of the rod; to do this it must pass over the South strut at a very acute angle, and at an even more acute one if it has to pass through a line-ring at West. When one imagines the heat which must be generated, and when one sees the wear which is inflicted on a cage strut which is not protected by a hardened line-guard, one must shudder at the wear imposed on the line itself.

My own solution to this is to get rid of the strut at South by careful sawing and filing. Admittedly in the first instance it takes some courage to mutilate a good reel in this way; however all my fly-reels have now had this treatment and I am able to give a positive assurance that the cages have suffered no noticeable loss of strength nor has the reels' efficiency been impaired in any way : what I do know is that my lines now last a great deal longer.

One manufacturer has made an attempt to overcome this problem by providing a roller instead of the strut at South, and this is fundamentally a sound idea, providing at least a halfway solution : however the roller in question is in three sections, of which the outer ones turn while the inner one is fixed, and this to my mind is self defeating; further, between the sections there must be sharp edges, and should any of these become proud as a result of wear it could spell havoc to a line.

LINE

For my own upstream Border fishing I now use a greased double-taper silk line. I say " now " advisedly, because at the time I first started fly fishing the modern lines of man-made fibres were just beginning to come onto the market and were the things to have; one gained the impression that silk lines were old-fashioned if not obsolescent and didn't really give them a second thought. My own conversion to silk came with the experience I have related earlier when I became convinced that to be more successful, particularly under thin water conditions, I must use a finer line. The necessity for also taking to an easier-actioned rod stemmed from this requirement, because the rod must be matched to the line: most fly fishermen choose their line to suit their rod, but I believe that this is the wrong way about, at any rate for those types of fly fishing where the thickness of line, and also the manner of its arrival on the water, can be a vital factor in avoiding alarm among the fish.

Some fishermen who mainly frequent larger waters may look askance at a quibble over a few thousandths of an inch, and point out that there are seven feet of leader between the line and the fly anyway: however my own experience tells me that these few thou' are of vital importance, especially in the case of the opaque plastic line with its hard and uncompromising outline and often glittering surface: in upstream Border fishing particularly, the line approaches the fish much more closely than the nominal length of the leader since, as I shall discuss later, it is necessary to throw an extremely loose line and leader if the ever-present problem of drag is to be avoided—this, of course, applies especially to dry flies. Further, we cannot only concern ourselves exclusively with the fish to which we are casting: in Border fishing it must always be taken for granted that the intervening water will be occupied by small fish who must not be panicked into rushing about and alarming their elders, and this is where the presentation and outline of the line itself is critical.

Silk lines are not only finer, as I propose to demonstrate, than the modern plastic coated lines of the same weight, but they actually appear finer still, and this appearance of fineness must be as apparent to the fishy eye as the human.

Silk lines are impregnated with linseed oil and receive as many as fourteen dressings of it over a manufacturing period of three to four months: any natural fibre which is oil-loaded must acquire translucency and any translucent object seen against the light, because of the shading off and blurring of its outline, must appear thinner than an object of similar shape which is opaque. To be fair some plastic coated lines do have a degree of translucence, but most are utterly opaque. If a length of line is laid along the surface of water, its weight will cause it to lie in a groove of its own making in the surface film; this groove is in effect an elongated lens, which, viewed from beneath magnifies the line into a small rope: it follows that even a slight difference in the thickness of the line, particularly if it has a hard outline, is proportionately magnified: there is no need to get under the water to prove this— one should only need to see the sun-shadow of a line on a shallow bottom to be convinced.

The classification of fly lines has been the source of more confusion than conversion to decimalisation. Originally, in the silk-only days, they were numbered through from " 1 "—the lightest trout line—to " 7 ", the heaviest salmon: this was fair enough because since the degree of taper was proportionate, the ratio of weight to thickness was always constant and one knew exactly where one was. Then, however, things began to get scientific and a new method of classification was superimposed based on the thickness of the line at its thinnest and thickest diameters and expressed in letters of the alphabet: " A " was the thickest trout line and the further down the alphabet you got, the thinner the piece of line, with " H " being about the finest; thus HCH represents a fairly standard double-taper line and HCF is a forward taper. GAAG would be a salmon line, the extra " A " in the middle indicating a degree of thickness greater than " A " by itself.

This was thrown into confusion in the first instance by the introduction of other fibres than silk into the braiding of fly lines, such as nylon, which is light in weight, and terylene, which is heavy: soon afterwards came the discovery that the specific gravity of a fly line could be determined by the plastic material with which it was coated rather than the fibre of which it was braided; first there came the so-called " bubble " lines which enabled a line to float without being greased, and then as a refinement to the older non-floating lines, the slow-sinking, the fast-sinking and the extra fast-sinking. It does not require a knowledge of physics to understand that a line which floats unaided must be lighter than a line of the same thickness which will sink like a stone : since it is the *weight* of the line which makes the rod work, the alphabet method of classification based on diameter can clearly no longer be relied upon to assist in matching a rod to a line and vice versa; a rod which works well with a sinking HCH would probably be a little too powerful to get the best out of a floating HCH.

A new classification has therefore come into use which is based on weight alone and ignores thickness : the latter factor leaves the new system less than perfect, but better minds than mine have been unable to come up with anything better, and until someone does I think it likely that both systems will continue side-by-side.

The newest classification takes us back to numbers again from " 12 "—the heaviest—down to " 1 ", the lightest (although in point of fact I know of no readily obtainable line lighter than ♯ 3); it is based on the weight in grains of the first ten yards of line, exclusive of the level tip prior to the commencement of the taper. The chief advantage of this is that a rod can be inscribed by the manufacturer with its appropriate " AFTM number " which is always preceded by the symbol " ♯ "—i.e. ♯ 6—and this indicates the actual weight of line with which the rod will perform best, regardless of thickness, taper or type. The packaging of the lines themselves carries an additional classification (back to letters again) indicating their type and purpose : " DT ", " WF " or " L " before the AFTM number tell you whether the line is " double-taper ", " weight-forward " (forward taper) or " level "; " F " or " S " after the AFTM number stand for " floating " or " sinking "; thus DT-6-F or WF-5-S.

I mentioned above that the old classification—letters and thickness—and the new—numbers and weight—may well continue side-by-side : " DT-6-F-HCH " although cumbersome, should exactly describe a line for type, characteristic, weight and diameter, and indeed does so in most respects except for the tip diameters in the letter classification; unfortunately these are just the dimensions with which in our context we are most concerned—and they are

virtually meaningless: the tips of *all* silk trout lines are " H ", and
similarly all plastic coated trout lines except the heavier sea trout
ones. Now the thinnest silk " H " is .023″ and thickest .032″; the
extremes in plastic coated " H " are .030″ and .036″; this at first
sight may seem fair enough until we remind ourselves that we are
covering the whole range of trout fly line tips from #3 to #8
and are working within an overall range of diameters embracing
less than .040″ altogether, including one " A " belly. Further, in
a given manufacturer's range of plastic coated lines one can, for
instance, find a .036″ tip on one line classified as " H " and the
same thickness in another tip shown as " G "; this when both
should truthfully be described as " F "! There is a published scale
of line thicknesses:

AA—.065″	D—.045″
A—.060″	E—.040″
B—.055″	F—.035″
C—.050″	G—.030″
	H—.025″

to which the mainly American manufacturers of plastic coated
lines and the British makers of silk lines for the most part adhere
as far as the bellies of their lines are concerned, to within two or
three thousandths of an inch: it seems not unreasonable to wonder
why the tips should not be so accurately designated, even if it in-
volves adjusting the scale and possibly adding another couple of
letters; instead we are given " G " as .030″ and " H " as .025″ but
find that in the actual plastic coated lines the nearest " G " is .036″
and the nearest " H " is .030″, and that the silk " H " is spread
over a range of nearly .010″.

I give below a table showing the approximate equivalents of
the various standards in double taper lines, but even these need not
necessarily be taken as applying exactly to all makes of line, since
" manufacturing tolerances " of up to 10% either way, especially
in the finer lines, are allowable in the new classification.

I have included only those line sizes which I know to be easily
available in this country at this time. The blanks *could* be filled in
by a process of arithmetical progression, but this would only create
confusion and one would be hard put to find a purpose for most
of the lines not included.

FLY LINE STANDARDS

| AFTM Nos. ‡ | Plastic coated nylon & terylene | | | | Silk Nos. |
| | Double taper | | Forward taper | | |
	Floating	Sinking	Floating	Sinking	
(1)					
(2)					
(3)					1
4	HEH		IEH		1
5	HDH		HDG		2
6	HCH	HEH	HCF	IEH	3
7	GBG	HDH	GBF	HDG	4
8	GAG	HCH	GAF	HCF	
9	GAAG	GBG	GAAF	GBF	5
10	G3AG	GAG	G3AF	GAF	
11	G4AG	GAAG			6
12					7

Trout fly lines, both double taper and forward taper, are normally thirty yards long: the level tip section is usually about
twenty-four inches in plastic coated and thirty-six inches in silk,
although this is sometimes greater in the heavier lines: the full
thickness is usually achieved in a further eight to twelve feet (six
to nine feet in sinking lines), this distance not normally being substantially less in forward tapers; in the types of line with which we
are most concerned in Border fishing—3, 4, 5 and 6 floating—
there is almost nothing in it between DT and FT in this first four
yards; in fact in some makes in these smaller sizes the greater
weight is actually in favour of the double taper: since the principle
of the forward taper cannot begin to be exploited until more than
ten yards of line are out of the top ring and the reverse taper has
begun, such a line, though excellent in bigger waters, is largely
superfluous in Border fishing. Since also a double taper line will
be reversed when the outer end has worn, and thus have two
lives to the forward taper's one, the former seems the obvious
choice.

One thing that my chart does show unequivocally is the advantage of silk in the matter of fineness, and in this respect I can
do no better than let the figures speak for themselves. A silk line
does need more looking after than a plastic coated one, but re-
sponds well, and if properly cared for will long outlast the other;
its dressing is not subject to the cracking to which the plastic coating is prone and, usually the more supple of the two to begin with,

a silk line tends to become even more supple with use, in contrast to the plastic. A silk line will be ruined if left on the reel through the winter, and while this practice is hardly to be recommended for any line, a plastic coated one would not be unduly affected. Ideally a silk line should be removed from the reel after each fishing excursion and not replaced until the next: I transfer mine to a line-winder as soon as I get home, cleaning it at the same time by running it through a soft cloth: prior to the next outing I replace it on the reel, at the same time greasing it by running it through an impregnated pad with a little extra treatment to the last four yards; this is normally sufficient to keep it floating all day. When a silk line is set aside for more than a short period, for example through the winter, it is best left coiled loosely in a capacious paper bag and stored where air can get at it. If the line exhibits a tendency to tackiness, either through old age or mis-treatment, this can often be checked, if not cured, by a generous dressing of baby powder.

For across-and-down wet fly fishing, which I normally only practice during the winter months for grayling and in the early spring for trout (the latter usually on a bigger river such as the Usk or the Teme) I almost always use a sinking line; this is quite simply because it catches more fish, who are lying and feeding deeper in rivers mostly carrying much more water than in summer. In fast-running water it is virtually impossible to fish deep with a floating line even with a very long leader and leaded flies; the flies, buoyed up by the current, will normally fish very little deeper than the end of the line, and thus a sinking line is a must.

While we are about it it is best to get a line which really does go down smartly and not teeter about on the surface for a time before it condescends to go under; my own preference is again for ungreased silk although a good fast-sinking plastic-coated tery-lene line is probably as good; considerations of fineness of tip are not as important as in fishing upstream with a floating line, since with downstream wet flies properly used the fish should always see the fly long before the line.

Beware of double tapered lines whose bellies sink much faster than their tips, for these will leave the flies waving about near the surface for much of the swim down: in exasperation I once cut off most of the taper from a line which did this and immediately started to catch fish. This, I think, makes a very good case in favour of a level line for downstream wet fly on Border rivers, for such a line is bound to sink evenly and is also, needless to say, much less expensive.

THE LEADER

I am not keen on using American terminology in fishing or any other subject where there is already a perfectly good English word; usually our word is shorter and just as descriptive—I have in mind " elevator " and " automobile " for instance. However the traditional English word for the length of tapered nylon or silkworm gut which separates the end of the fly line from the fly is the " cast "; although shorter by two letters than " leader " I find it not only undescriptive but capable of getting confused with the verb of the same name which describes the act of getting the fly to the fish; therefore as far as I am concerned " leader " it is.

For Border fishing a simple tapered leader of a length not greater than that of the rod is all that is necessary or indeed desirable: tapered leaders are either a series of lengths of level nylon of reducing thickness tied together by means of blood knots, or else " knotless tapers "; the latter, of course must be bought, whereas the former can be made up very cheaply and in quantity from five or six spools of nylon of an appropriate variety of diameters. A difference of thickness greater than .002" is not desirable between adjacent strands, particularly in the finer diameters: apart from this cheapness, the only other advantage to a made-up leader is that it can be constructed to whatever dimensions the tier may determine; its main disadvantage, apart from the fact that it is not so much a continuous taper as a series of low steps, is in its knots; each extra knot in a leader is a tangle hazard, particularly under windy conditions; a leader turning over in the air and sliding along another part of itself may do so with impunity until the slide is checked by a knot; when this happens it is odds-on that it will tie another knot of its own—a wind knot; a wind knot usually takes the form of a simple half-hitch, than which there is no more efficient reducer of the breaking strain of nylon; if you don't believe me get hold of a length of fairly strong nylon—say 12 lb. b.s.—and having wrapped some of it round each hand try to break it; you will find yourself in danger of a nasty cut if you persist; now tie a simple half-hitch wind knot in the middle of it and try again; this simple experiment should convince anyone that wind knots must not be tolerated under any circumstances; the leader should be examined at frequent intervals during fishing, and if a wind knot is found either the offending piece of nylon should be discarded or the wind knot should be unravelled (this is usually possible, with the aid of two pins, provided the knot has not been allowed to exist long enough to get itself drawn up too tightly).

While the blood knots of which a made-up leader is formed are quite the most efficient means of joining nylon monofilament, and at the same time impose the least reduction on its breaking strain, each must be regarded as a danger point, particularly when self-tied : professionally tied blood knots are likely to be more reliable, but any error in their tying, particularly when drawing-up, can drastically reduce their efficiency. To sum up, then, all unessential knots should be avoided in a leader, and this brings us back to the continuous knotless taper, which in my view is worth every penny of the few extra shillings that it costs.

One reads of carefully calculated compound—even reversed—tapers, but these are applicable only in certain specialised forms of fly fishing where extremely long casting combined with long leaders may be required : for reservoir fishing, for example, I have come across formulae for leaders of fifteen or sixteen feet; here obviously some sort of compound taper is needed in order to try and get the leader to turn over properly and straighten when the final forward cast is made. Correct turning over and straightening in Border fishing is largely achieved by the correct balance of the outfit combined with the skill of the caster, but is likely to be assisted by a leader of fairly steep taper : this requirement in the leader—a steep taper—can more readily be understood if one accepts that there should be a continuous and steady taper right through the outfit from the casting elbow to the fly. There should not be too great a step at the point where the line and the leader join, and therefore the butt diameter of the leader must be as close as possible to the tip diameter of the line; here again the use of a silk line helps us, because the tip thickness of a Border weight silk line is in the region of .026″, whereas that of an equivalent " bubble " line can be nearly .010″ more : on a silk line therefore a leader butt diameter would ideally be about .022″—the equivalent of 25-30 lb. b.s. nylon; however I know of no knotless taper trout casts which come quite as thick as this; .018″ is about the maximum obtainable and in practice this proves entirely satisfactory; a perfectionist might decide to blood-knot a six inch length of .022″ nylon onto the butt of his knotless leader, but I doubt if much difference would be noticed and the extra blood knot could represent an extra tangle hazard.

There has to be at least one blood knot on our leader, and that is between the tip of the leader and the " point "; the point is a length (say eighteen inches) of fine level nylon between the tip of the leader and the fly. If one does not employ a point but ties the fly direct to the tapered leader, it is only a matter of time before the leader is so eroded by fly changes that the tip is much thicker than is desirable and the whole leader must be discarded; on the other hand a leader whose point is changed occasionally (at *least* every outing) can be made to last an economically long time. Another argument in favour of a separate point is that I have found that the best presentation of the fly is achieved by using a leader of fairly stiff nylon but a point of much softer material : different brands of nylon, both in tapered leader form and level spools, display surprising variations of stiffness, and this is worth careful investigation before purchasing : as far as the level point is concerned it is worth noting that the limpest nylons are the ones most favoured by coarse fishing match anglers. The value of stiffness in the main leader is in its ability to turn over and straighten even under windy conditions; a main leader of limp nylon will fall about all over the place in these circumstances; on the other hand stiffness is not a desirable feature in a point, since it can lend an unnatural movement to the fly; it will also transmit drag much more quickly than a soft point, since the latter leaves the fly much freer to drift at the behest of the current.

Assuming that we are using a seven-foot rod, the overall length of our leader should not be greater than seven feet six inches at the most : since the point will be about eighteen inches, the length of the main leader must be six feet. We have established that the butt diameter must be as great as possible and will probably be in the region of .018″ : what about the other end? Tip sizes of fly leaders are usually still expressed as 5X, 4X, 3X, 2X, 1X and so on : this is a hang-over from the days before nylon monofilament when leaders were made of drawn silkworm gut; the " X " as in arithmetic means " times ", and the figure signifies the number of times the gut has been drawn (and therefore scraped) through holes of diminishing diameter. The thickness of nylon is usually expressed in thousandths of an inch which is also related to its reputed breaking strain, which is normally the dry breaking strain; here we encounter a variant, because some manufacturers are more optimistic than others about the breaking strain of their products: I give below an approximate conversion table for the various classifications.

Size	Diameter	Approx. b.s.	Size	Diameter	Approx. b.s.
8X	.0045″	1½ lb.	OX	.011″	7 lb.
7X	.005″	1¾ lb.	9/5	.012″	8¼ lb.
6X	.0055″	2 lb.	8/5	.013″	9 lb.
5X	.006″	2½ lb.	7/5	.014″	11 lb.
4X	.007″	3¼ lb.	6/5	.015″	13 lb.
3X	.008″	4½ lb.	4/5	.017″	18 lb.
2X	.009″	5 lb.	3/5	.019″	19 lb.
1X	.010″	6 lb.	1/5	.021″	22 lb.

The breaking strains on this table refer to conventional nylon and not the new so-called " strong " nylon: it is claimed for the latter that it is much finer for its breaking strain (or, put another way, that it has a higher breaking strain for its relative diameter) and that it has a greater resistance to breakage at the knots; however, being also less elastic than the older type of nylon, it absorbs less of the energy of an over-enthusiastic strike, so should be used with caution by those, like me, whose reactions are not always under icy control.

Natural silkworm gut is so rarely obtainable these days that discussion of it is largely academic: that it was an excellent leader material in its day is beyond dispute, although it suffered from serious disadvantages; I doubt that, even were it still freely available, it would rank as a serious rival to the increasing efficiency of nylon monofilament. It is claimed that it is less visible in water than nylon and this may well be true, since, unlike nylon it absorbs water; indeed, before it can be used safely it must be kept soaked in water to overcome its tendency to stiffness and brittleness, and this is one of its disadvantages; once soaked, however, it is remarkably supple—perhaps too much so for a dry fly main leader. Another disadvantage is that it is not safely " drawn " to less that 4X, and of course nylon leaders can be freely obtained down to 7X. Further I have a feeling that whoever made the first conversions of the " X " tables from gut to nylon was guided by breaking strains rather than diameters: I still have in my possession a dozen high quality gut casts " drawn to 3X "; the tip diameter of all these is exactly .010″, which is, of course 1X and 6 lb. breaking strain by the above table. Finally there are no continuous knotless tapers in gut, and leaders had to be made up of a number of graded strands, knotted together.

However to get back to our own, Border fishing, leader: I find personally that for general use under average conditions my best point size is 4X or about $3\frac{1}{4}$ lb. b.s.; in conditions of thin clear water and with a small fly I will come down to 2 lb. b.s. and in heavy or coloured water and on the Mayfly I will rise to 4 lb. Ideally therefore a $3\frac{1}{4}$ lb. or 4X point should be attached to a leader whose tip size is not more than .002″ greater, and this gives us 3X or 2X; our requirement for this leader then, is one of six feet tapered to 3X or 2X; the fact that we are reducing our diameter from .018″ down to .008″ or .009″ within the space of six feet ensures compliance with the initially stated requirement of a fairly steep taper.

In choosing leader material, consideration should be given to the light reflecting properties of the various makes of nylon offered: some makes, ideal in other ways, possess a high degree of glitter, especially in sunlight; needless to say these should be avoided, since if *we* can see them gleaming, how much more so can the fish, particularly when the leader is under water.

The leader described above will serve for all normal purposes in Border fishing, whether the method be upstream dry fly or nymph or a single downstream wet fly. However on the odd larger river, where two or three wet flies are to be fished downstream, a longer rod will be employed as mentioned earlier: this will ideally be about nine feet long, so that the leader also should be about that length; nevertheless the same basic main leader can be used; the three flies should be spaced about eighteen inches apart so that the dropper of the " bob " fly—the top one, nearest the rod tip— will correspond with the tip of the six foot main leader; the middle dropper will be eighteen inches further down and the point fly eighteen inches beyond that. I am aware that the conventional distance between wet flies is usually stated as three feet, but that is for larger waters and should not even then be regarded as arbitrary: however should a greater interval than eighteen inches be wanted on a nine foot leader, it can be achieved either by dispensing with the middle fly or else making up a leader with less than six feet between the line and the first dropper, but this will have the effect of making the flies fish closer to the surface.

A length of leader greater than that of the rod should be avoided if possible unless one has complete confidence that the union between the line and the leader—particularly if it is knot-to-loop and not loop-to-loop—can pass and repass the top ring of the rod quite freely and without check; many a good fish has smashed the leader and regained his freedom because of this.

The attachment of the droppers is often a source of concern to many anglers: on a ready-made wet-fly leader the dropper-links are formed by leaving one of the loose ends of each of the completed blood knots untrimmed; however the time will come when the process of fly changing will have shortened the dropper-link so much that it is no longer possible to tie a fly on it, and another link is required. My own method of doing this is to tie a one-inch loop in a six-inch length of nylon; I then fold this loop round the main leader above the blood knot and pass the loose end through it, forming a slip knot; the so-formed double loop round the main leader, and the double nylon on nearly the first inch of dropper-link, both help to make the latter stand out well, and I find this more satisfactory than the tucked half-blood knot more commonly employed. A dropper-link should not be more than five inches, and with the possible exception of the top dropper or bob fly, should be as short as it can conveniently be made.

The conventional method of attaching the leader to the end of the line is by means of a tucked sheet bend, more frequently called the " figure-of-eight ": this knot is of course in the line and not the leader, which should already have a loop at its butt end: if this loop is not present, or if one is making up one's own leader, it should be formed by a blood bight knot, which has a high breakage resistance, and *not* a double overhand, which does not.

A far more satisfactory method of joining leader to line, and one which can very rapidly be undone, is the loop-to-loop union referred to above: for this it is necessary to make a permanent loop in the end of the line, and here again the silk line scores because its narrowness allows of little increase in bulk. It is best first to strip the leading two inches of line of dressing, and this can be done with a sharp knife used edgeways as a scraper; the stripped portion is then folded back upon itself forming a one-inch loop; this is then tightly whipped with a fine strong thread—stocking-darning nylon is ideal—until a loop remains of about a quarter of an inch or perhaps a little more; care should be taken in taper-ing the rear end of this binding, where it passes over the cut end of the line, to ensure that no step or protrusion remains which could hinder the passage of the loop through the top ring of the rod. Finally the whole binding should be impregnated with a thin waterproof glue or with rod varnish. A more efficient means of stripping the dressing from the end two inches of line is to em-ploy amyl acetate on the plastic-coated variety and a bland paint-stripper on oil-dressed silk: however great care should be taken in the use of these substances, firstly to ensure that none gets on any other part of the line and secondly to wash away all trace once the softened dressing has been scraped off. To attach the leader to the line one simply passes the loop of the leader through the loop in the line and then puts the leader through its own loop; the completed union should look like a neat reef knot without loose ends, and will pass and repass a small top ring without difficulty.

On the subject of how best to attach a fly to the point of the leader I have seen grown and intelligent men come to the verge of fisticuffs: purists aver that one sort of knot should be used for a dry fly and another sort for a wet; personally I have tried every sort of knot whose use I have seen recommended, and nowadays I use one single knot for all flies and all conditions—a four-turn half-blood—to my entire satisfaction; sometimes I will risk three turns if I am using a particularly small fly and am not anticipating an outsize fish.

I am firmly of the opinion that more important than the knots themselves is the method of tying them, and in particular of draw-ing them up: I prefer the expression " drawing up " rather than " tightening " because it is important not to over-tighten, which can be seriously weakening; especially in the case of the various blood knots it is necessary to wind the turns evenly and under even tension, so that when the knot is drawn up the stresses are evenly distributed; this can be greatly facilitated by the liberal impregna-tion of the knot with spit to lubricate it before drawing up; whenever possible before forming a blood knot I prefer to hold both ends of nylon in my mouth for a short time in order to soften and lubricate them.

ACCESSORIES

So far we have dealt with those items of tackle which are essential in delivering the fly to the fish. There is also a long list of accessory items of varying degrees of importance which assist in the exercise of fly fishing : however, once one is in possession of the basic outfit—rod, reel, line, leader and of course flies, one is in a position to start fishing; everything else is supporting equipment and as such not absolutely essential, although I would personally hesitate to begin fishing without waders and landing net. It is only human nature for the enthusiastic newcomer to the sport to over-equip himself, so that once the basic outfit has been achieved I believe that one should look critically at every other item of equipment and decide just how essential it is. Nor do I advocate the other extreme, as practised by one or two of my acquaintance, of pulling on a pair of waders over the clothes they stand up in and sallying forth for a day's fishing with a spare spool of point nylon and a few flies in a matchbox; this may be delightfully simple but contingencies have a habit of arising. I have found that the best practice is to have a fishing jacket—in my case an ex-army combat jacket—with everything I require permanently in it so that nothing essential gets left behind. When I carry a haversack it is a small one and its primary purpose is to contain my sandwiches, something to drink and a light waterproof; if I keep the odd fish it will go into it too, in a polythene bag.

LANDING NET. Some Border fishermen dispense with a landing net, arguing that any fish they are likely to catch will not be large enough to justify one. Such thinking deserves to lose a few decent fish and is not in my view to be encouraged. Should a good fish be encountered it will often need to be played to exhaustion before it can be tailed or gilled, but my main concern is with undersized fish which will be returned; a wet net is the ideal thing in which to handle them to avoid damage to their mucus coating which is so essential to their continued well-being. The type of landing net and frame is not material : care should be taken if choosing one of the models which collapse completely, since one which performs admirably in the tackle shop may refuse to open at a critical moment at the water, often because a mesh has so arranged itself that it binds one of the working parts. The only completely fool-proof landing net frame is the fixed type, which is also much cheaper, and I find that a sixteen inch three-fold (triangular) frame is adequate for Border fishing requirements.

As a result of losing an argument in the late war I am left with only one leg of my own, the other being government issue: I therefore use my landing-net frame in conjunction with a stout four-foot bamboo handle of the type favoured by coarse fishermen, which doubles as a wading staff. Apart from the much greater ease in netting a lively fish which the longer reach provides, I can re-commend this type of landing net cum wading staff for Border fishing even to those who are more sure-footed than I. I would not advocate wading for the sake of it, in fact for reasons which I shall give later, I believe that it should be avoided if at all possible: however in most Border waters this is more easily said than done, and it is frequently not possible to fish without wad-ing; and on waters where a very lively current combines with an uneven, slippery or rocky bottom—or a combination of all three— a wading staff can be a great comfort. Mine is furnished with a large metal ring which is free to run up and down the shaft, and this is connected to my left shoulder by a piece of catapult elastic of approximately the length of my arm: thus at any time I can have both arms free and my net trailing behind me, disregarded and without fear of getting lost; should it get itself caught up in the bushes during my forward progress, it lets me know about it with a gentle tugging as the elastic takes up the strain instead of pulling me over backwards as would a length of unresilient cord. The butt end of my staff is fitted with a rubber stick-pad; this serves the triple purpose of reducing noise as it drags on stony ground, sealing the end and preventing the sliding ring from coming off the shaft.

The net itself will repay critical selection; the insistence of a great number of game fishermen that their landing net should be of variegated black-and-yellow cord is a source of quiet amuse-ment in the tackle trade; such nets, though well made are never-theless of cotton, and as such short lived due to a propensity to rot. Far more serviceable and almost indestructible, to say nothing of cheaper, is nylon: a word of warning here though: a *yellow* nylon net should be avoided; this will have been steeped in linseed oil and will tend to become harder and more wiry in use, so much so that a fish held in it for unhooking and returning can be badly scraped: a green nylon landing net, which derives its colour from its being soaked in copper napthanate, is ideal; this becomes progressively softer in use, and when it is laid in the water a fish drawn over it is less likely to panic than when confronted with yellow nylon or variegated cotton. Many landing nets these days, particularly nylon, are made by machine, but this need be no detraction; indeed a good machine-made net can be far superior from a functional point of view than a poor hand-made one. Hand-made nets usually have progressively larger meshes from bottom to top, and in some the meshes near the neck are large enough for a moderate fish to slip through if netted awkwardly: a machine-made net cannot suffer from this disability since all its meshes are the same throughout, and in addition, since it is rectangular in shape and not tapered, is assured of a good bag in the bottom.

WADERS

Accepting that thigh waders are a necessary item for the regular Border fisherman, we are at once confronted with the problem of reconciling seemingly opposed requirements—silence and safety: this would not be so were it still possible to obtain waders with rigid-backed felt soles, but it is years since I have seen these advertised. I well remember meeting a fellow angler on a day in high summer when the water was very low and gin clear: one of his remarks has stayed in my mind ever since; it was: " you need to wear carpet slippers if you want to get within twenty yards of these fish!" What he had in mind was the ease with which fish can be alarmed by underwater sound, which I find, contrary to an earlier assumption, carries almost as well upstream as down except in the roughest water. I recall a peculiarly graphic example of this when I was fishing the Hindwell Brook in N.W. Herefordshire: the water was neither low nor unusually clear, and the current was strong; I was moving quietly upstream in a dark tunnel of overhanging foliage, the upstream end of which was closed with similar foliage except for a small gap perhaps eighteen inches square through which I could see a small trout, lying in the sunlight of the open water above my tunnel, at least fifteen yards upstream of me; he could not possibly see me and it was only because of a trick of the light that I could see him, lazily finning, unperturbed. My toe stubbed, not hard, against a rock, and in the instant that fish was gone.

A simple answer to this might appear to be the wearing of gum boot-type soft soled waders, but this I cannot recommend in the interest of safety since they are treacherously slippy, especially on alga covered underwater rocks: in the absence of rigid felt soles the only really safe wader is one with rigid nailed soles; only these give reasonable stability on slippery rocks and an even distribution of load on treacherous bottoms comprising a firm surface layer over soft mud; gumboot-type waders with studs riveted into the soles are not nearly so satisfactory since they are still soft soled. However, nailed waders are an obvious source of noise on any bottom except mud or clay, so that our dilemma is clear; the only answer is to wade with the greatest circumspection, studying to put down each foot as quietly as possible, and above all to do so slowly. In this way also surface ripples can be reduced to a minimum; these outward spreading rings are often not taken into account by the Border fisherman, in the belief that they are swamped by the current and so prevented from spreading upstream; this is true only in fairly fast water, and I believe that wading ripples can run counter to the stream, and though not noticeable to the angler are visible to the fish who will be alerted by the unnatural change in the surface pattern.

There is another reason why unessential wading should be avoided : every step that is taken disturbs or destroys some link in the river's food chain; often enough it will be nymphs or other small animals on the undersides of stones which are trodden on or kicked : invariably, though, there will be displacement of the algal film which covers the bed of the stream and which provides the food of these small creatures. One can often see where another fisherman has recently waded by his lighter footmarks in the darker stream bed; each of those lighter patches represents an area of alga which has been washed away, and as I have mentioned earlier few Border streams are so well endowed with nourishment that any potential source of food should needlessly be destroyed.

Even in those places where wading can be avoided, progress along the riverside in nailed boots (or for that matter any other sort of footwear, including carpet slippers) should be made with care: although the crunch of bankside shingle does not reach a fish with quite such amplified clarity as the same sound originating in the bed of the stream, the sensitive lateral line of the fish can be expected to pick up most ground noises above a fairly low level; the thump of a heavy footfall and the clatter of displaced stones in particular are sounds which upstream fish can register at surprising distances.

SCISSORS are not really an essential to an angler who still has his own teeth, although they can be rather more precise for trimming the loose end of a knot; for this purpose, however, I prefer that type of nail-clipper which is like a pair of lightweight side-cut pliers, because in an emergency they can be used for cutting through a hook. By " emergency " I mean the occasion when part of one's anatomy (usually an ear or finger, but I have known of nose and lip, among other places) becomes well hooked: in this situation many a victim has struggled painfully to withdraw the hook, or else abandoned his fishing to go and seek a doctor; frequently, however, the whole performance can be short-circuited by the simple progress of pushing the hook further through, so that the point emerges, and cutting it off behind the barb, which is where the side-cut nail clipper comes in handy.

AMADOU. An accessory which I regard as of great value though not absolutely essential is my pad of amadou: this is a dried fungus which comes in small sheets and looks rather like chamois leather. The characteristic of amadou is its power of water absorbtion, and a waterlogged dry fly pressed between its folds will immediately return to its dehydrated state; it has long been used by the dental profession as a styptic because of this and indeed in a recent period of short supply I was only able to get a bit through a dentist friend. Although by its nature rather fragile, a piece of amadou can be made to last indefinitely if properly treated : mine is mounted on a piece of canvas about three inches by four inches, to which size it had already been trimmed; it is attached to the canvas by means of a contact adhesive at the edges only, and the whole thing folds into a compact wallet of three inches by two.

Since I lost my last one by dropping it in the river my present amadou pad is attached to me by means of a length of strong cord and a swivel; I have seen others with a buttonhole tab extension to the canvas attached to a convenient coat button.

HOOK SHARPENER. This is one small accessory without which I would be reluctant to go fishing. In the enclosed conditions which for the most part obtain in Border fishing the hook point is subject to constant blunting in consequence of frequent involvement with sticks and stones, and a hook not used for some time will almost certain to be found on examination to have acquired a patina of rust: a burred or blunted or rusty hook-point may easily make the difference between a fish landed and a fish lost or missed, and an angler who casts a fly whose hook he is not satisfied is needle sharp is unnecessarily weighting the scales against himself. My own stone is a sliver of medium grade Carborundum, about one inch by three-eights of an inch, with a thickness of one-eighth inch tapering to about one-twelfth inch; this thinness is important since it enables one to work right round the hook point, although a sharpener which can only get at the underside of the hook is better than none at all. A useful sharpener can be made by glueing a strip of emery cloth to a sliver of wood—a redundant lolly stick is ideal. In touching up a hook I find it best to stroke the sharpener towards the bend, for this ensures that the point is left clean of swarf; in short-point hooks with the barb close to the point (which I think are the best) there is usually a knife-edge between the point and the tip of the barb, and this can be kept sharp by backward and diagonal strokes of the stone.

FLY FLOATANT. For floating my dry flies I use a saturated solution of solid Mucilin (not silicone) line grease in commercial carbon tetrachloride: the latter is available quite cheaply at most chemists and is a well-known dry-cleaning agent. I half fill a small wide-necked polythene jar with the fluid and go on putting in slivers of grease until no more will dissolve; final dissolution can take a few hours. The fly is dipped in this solution, given a shake and a blow, and allowed to dry, which takes a minute or so; it is now coated all over and impregnated with an efficient flotant, but will not dispense an oil film on the water around it; further it will float all day without a further dunking unless it should happen to be sampled by quite a lot of fish; if all dry flies are immersed in advance it is not, therefore, strictly necessary to take the flotant along at all. I do not favour the use of silicones as flotants since they tend to seal the exterior of the fly without penetrating the body: many modern anglers overlook the fact that not a few traditional fly dressings take into account the effect on the body material when impregnated with oil; the classic example of this must be the Greenwell's Glory—yellow bodied when first dressed, translucent olive after oiling.

DEGREASER. In Border fishing it is often necessary to change continually from dry fly to nymph and back again. With a dry fly the leader must float. I have seen the opposite postulated on more than one occasion but for the life of me I cannot see how it is managed; perhaps it is possible in chalk stream fishing, but as far as I am concerned if my leader sinks my fly is very soon dragged after it. Now of course a nymph *must* sink, smartly and without fuss; but it cannot do so if the leader, or at any rate the point, is buoyant. With the dry fly, if the leader shows a predisposition to sink, this is quickly remedied with a smear of line grease or even a quick rub across a sweaty nose: but with the nymph the problem of ensuring that the point sinks is less easily disposed of, since there are more factors combining to keep it floating; one of these is the deliberate act just mentioned, another is the transfer of natural grease from the fingers when handling the fly; more serious is the transfer of line flotant from a greased silk line, and this is one of the few points where the bubble line scores over silk. However with forethought this problem can be reduced to minimal proportions, and the first thing is to try and remember only to handle the line with the minimum number of fingers and to wipe those frequently on the front of your jacket or anywhere else convenient: when it is necessary to handle the leader at all, it is a wise precaution to moisten the fingers concerned with saliva or mud, so that it is these which are transferred to the leader and not any residue of grease which may be lurking underneath. Eventually though there comes a time when these simple precautions and remedies are not effective, and the leader, or that portion of it which is required to sink, must be degreased: I find that this is best done by carrying a small pad soaked in a strong solution of domestic washing-up liquid, in the proportion of about four parts

of water to one of detergent, in an easily opened but watertight
container; it is a simple matter occasionally to run the leader
through this pad, at the same time using it to decontaminate the
fingers; remember, though, to rinse or at least wipe the hands
afterwards, as a residue of detergent transferred to the line, be it
greased or bubble, can have the same effect as on the leader.

Another efficient degreasing device—for which we have to thank
Richard Walker, from whom so many sensible ideas have stemmed
—is to make a mixture of neat washing-up liquid and Fuller's
earth to the consistency of a lump of Plasticene : the leader needs
only to be drawn through this lump in order to make it sink in-
stantly. As with putty, the mixture should be sufficiently stiff as
not to separate and stick to the fingers when it is handled.

DISGORGER. It is always a wise precaution to carry some form of
disgorger, the more humanely to remove an awkwardly placed
hook from a fish which is to be returned. Probably the most
efficient type is a pair of surgical artery forceps, although these
need using with caution if damage to the dressing of the fly is to
be avoided; artery forceps have very sharp teeth which are still
effectual even if the points are filed, so that care should be taken
to grip the hook at the bend, behind the dressing, if the fly is not
to be ruined : safer in this respect is the ring-type disgorger, whose
end is like that of a small button-hook only with the hook bent
sideways to an angle of ninety degrees; the common fork-type disgorger is not to be recommended since it too easily damages the
fish.

Small fish hooked around the front of the mouth can often be
unhooked without removing them from the water : this is done
by grasping the fly between the forefinger and thumb and imparting a sharp up-and-down shake; nine times out of ten this will be
effective and the fish will depart with less discomfort than if he
had been netted and formally unhooked; but this particular ploy
should not be tried when the hook is inside the mouth, or if the
fish is well hooked in the scissors when it is only too easy to
tear away the maxillary—the long bony plate which covers the
scissors.

If a fish has gorged the fly, and it is embedded so far back in
the throat that damage is bound to result from any attempt at its
removal, it is far better either to kill the fish out of hand or else

to release it to get rid of the fly in its own way, as assuredly it will; if the latter course is adopted obviously the nylon should be cut as near as possible to the fly, or even the shank of the hook itself behind the eye—this is often possible with the side-cut clippers I described earlier. One thing is certain: if any blood shows as a result of back-of-the-mouth hooking the fish may be regarded as doomed, for his chances of recovery are minimal even if he swims away apparently none the worse.

SHOT & WIRE. A fish is often encountered in Border fishing—frequently a good grayling—who won't bother to come up to your offering and to whom it seems impossible, because of the speed of the current or some other factor, to get a nymph deep enough: this dilemma can often be overcome by adding extra weight to the fly, and many anglers carry a card of fuse-wire or similar against such a contingency; this they wind on around the head of the fly. Nearly all my Border nymphs are weighted anyway under the dressing, but in addition I like to have a few split-shot in my pocket—size 6 or 8 (what the coarse fishermen calls "dust shot"): when the occasion demands I nip one of these—two sometimes—on the point about an inch from the fly, and find that this is as effective to the purpose as anything.

FLY RETRIEVER. No one can suggest that "essential equipment" would embrace a device for rescuing a fly which has got itself securely tied to an out-of-reach branch; indeed with shop flies so ridiculously cheap many fishermen will break off several in a day and think nothing of it. However when enthusiastic and pains-taking effort have gone into the production of a self-tied master-piece it is not so easy lightly to abandon it, and for the benefit of those who do have a paternal reluctance to leaving their creations in trees, without at least some attempt at retrieving them, I will now describe two gadgets which I have found useful. Incident-ally no fly should be so abandoned if it is at all possible to re-trieve it: I am thinking in particular of many that I see where the leader rather than the fly has become entangled and the fly is left dangling in the breeze; such lures are often irresistible to birds, with predictable and tragic consequences.

My first device is only of value to those who, like me, employ a wading staff consisting of a landing handle whose end is furnished with a socket containing a standard screw thread—standard, that is, to the fishing tackle industry. Into this can be screwed what is known as a weed-cutter or weed scythe, of which several patterns are available, some with straight blades, some curved: the sharpened edge is towards the holder, but some of the blades are angled away from him, and some towards him, and it is the latter type whose cutting edge makes a slightly acute angle with the pole which is the effective one for our purpose: provided the edge is kept sharp this will cut through thin branches to a height of five feet above the head of the wielder if drawn sharply downward.

The second gadget gives a rather longer reach and costs virtually nothing since it is home made: one requires a metal skewer of the type which is also offered as a tent peg, a length of plastic-covered, rigid but easily bendable wire such as is sold for gardening purposes, and about four yards of strong cord. The skewer is first bent into a wide hook; one end of the wire is then fixed firmly to it so that the free end comes off the hook just above the " eye " and finally the cord is attached by one end to the eye. The method of employment is to thread the loose end of the wire down through the first two or three rings of the rod (which is why the wire should be plastic covered); this should leave the hook standing upright above the top ring: the rod is then held by the butt and manoeuvred so that the hook can be placed over the offending branch, it having first been ascertained that the branch is sufficiently pliable for our purpose; with the hook in position the rod can be withdrawn and set aside. It remains now only to haul on the cord until the fly can be reached by hand, or else with our weed scythe if we happen to have that with us as well. The question now remaining is: how to retrieve the hook? This is surprisingly easy; the cord is drawn down once more and then released sharply, and this should catapult the hook clear of the branch.

Resort to exercises such as are described above would often be unnecessary if snatching were avoided: it is quite true that a fly cast over a branch can often tie the leader in an extraordinarily efficient knot, but it does not always do so; frequently it is the ensuing snatch or hard pull which jams the fly inextricably. If, when the fly is seen to be caught up, the caster draws the line delicately, the fly can often be retrieved from quite a " cat's cradle "; this is particularly so with a dry fly, since careful handling can leave the hackles masking the hook. If the caught-up fly is within reach of the rod tip it is often possible to free it by winching in until the fly is just outside the top ring, when upward or sideways pressure may do the trick.

OVERTROUSERS. Lastly, and by no means facetiously, I commend to the intending Border fisherman the purchase of a pair of really stout waterproof overtrousers. I can offer it as a statistical fact that I catch more fish from a sitting position than from all others combined—a sitting position in which I may have waited for ten or fifteen minutes to observe and allow fish to settle, and one to reach which I may have found it necessary to toboggan down a muddy, brambly bank on my backside. My own are made of reinforced P.V.C., and will resist sharp stones and thorns and enable me to sit down anytime and anywhere—in a puddle if necessary. My friends and I have evolved simple modifications to the overtrousers as we buy them, to convert them into what we call " rompers ": to make movement easier we cut them off at the knee (they are worn outside the waders to prevent rain and debris running down into the boot), and we furnish them with rudimentary braces; as supplied, overtrousers are usually elastic-waisted, and can settle on the hips to the point where the lowered crutch can interfere with free movement, especially if bought on the large side, which is desirable if not elegant.

Chapter Three

NATURAL FLIES

UNPALATABLE AS is may be to the purist, the most successful artificial fly at any given time on a Border stream is likely to be a
general pattern—that is a fly which imitates no specific natural insect but which suggests any one of a considerable number. This is
not to be disrespectful to the purist; indeed I think that many of
us have from time to time a sneaking envy of him, and would like
occasionally an opportunity of being purists ourselves or at any
rate to be able to fish in places where it is possible, even necessary,
to be a purist.

There are three main reasons for the pre-eminence of the general
pattern on Border waters. Two I have already given; namely the
dearth of regular hatches of large numbers of specific species, and
the general inadequacy of food supplies which makes anything eat-
able worth considering. The third is the speed, general turmoil
and often colour of the water; there is rarely the opportunity for
a leisurely inspection of a prospective morsel in ideal conditions
of light before it is whipped away beyond recall: the Border fish,
therefore, has to make up his mind fairly smartly.

Now I don't want to give the impression, in spite of what I
have already written, that a Border fish will gobble anything that
comes along; very much to the contrary; he can be, and often is,
almost as selective in his own way as his chalk stream cousin,
although his range of acceptability is broader. The use of an artificial fly exactly imitating (in the fly dresser's opinion) a specific
insect *may* hit the nail on the head first time; it is more likely not
to: a general pattern which gives an impressionistic suggestion of
a number of likely insects (in the fish's opinion) is more assured
of success. Since it has never been possible to canvas the opinions

of the fish (except empirically, by making a continuous succession of offerings over a period of many lifetimes) it is difficult to be convincing on why some general patterns are so successful; certainly many of them appear to bear little resemblance to any known insect, at any rate in the eye of the human beholder: why, for instance, is the use of the Dogsbody so often profitable whenever the fish are feeding on the black gnat?

A detailed entomological study of the insects frequenting Border streams, therefore, is not called for in the context of fish-catching efficiency: a general understanding of the life cycles of the aquatic orders of insects, and the ability to recognise non- or semi-aquatic specimens at order level is normally sufficient, though the observant angler will quickly begin to identify actual species where they occur often enough on his own stretch of water. By " order " I mean one of the twenty-four divisions into which the insect class is divided; it is the point of division at which types of insect are clearly recognisable as different from other types; thus the order *Plecoptera* comprises the stoneflies, *Trichoptera* is the sedges, and *Ephemeroptera* the up-winged flies of which the mayfly is the largest and best known.

Within the Terms of Reference of this book, therefore, I propose to deal with natural insects in a general way only; at the same time I have no desire to persuade anyone that a more comprehensive interest in angling entomology is not deeply rewarding. For the fisherman—and I think that this will apply to most Border fly fishermen—whose interest in the sport extends beyond the mere catching of fish, the study of the insects which comprise the indispensable third side of his sporting triangle can be as fascinating as the sport itself; indeed I know of several happy anglers who will leave their rods leaning against a fence and go off " bug hunting " whenever the fishing is a little slow. Two excellent works on this subject are Harris's " Angler's Entomology "[1] and John Goddard's " Trout Fly Recognition ";[2] A word of warning, though, to prospective aquatic entomologists on Border streams, on a theme which I have to come back to all too frequently: almost without exception the books on this subject divide themselves into two parts; the first, and infinitely larger one will prob-

[1] " An Angler's Entomology "; J. R. Harris, F.R.E.S., M.A. (Dublin), New Naturalist Library; Collins, London.
[2] " Trout Fly Recognition "; John Goddard; A. & C. Black, London.

ably be headed " Ephemeroptera "; the second part will be called simply " other insects ". Let it not be forgotten that as far as we Border fishermen are concerned both the order and the balance of importance must be reversed.

The insects of the riverside can be divided into three types: aquatic, semi-aquatic and terrestrial. Aquatic insects are those who are born in the water, live and breed in, on or over it, and finally die in, on or near it: semi-aquatic insects are, as the name implies, those who spend most of their time aquatically but who leave the water at some time in their life cycle, say to lay eggs or to pupate on land: terrestrial insects are those which are not aquatic; that is to say that they can be found anywhere whether there is water or not, although there are many species whose preference for damp places leads them to be more common at the riverside.

These divisions are largely academic, especially to the dry fly fisherman, since it makes little difference to him whether the fly on the water has flown or fallen onto it or come up from beneath the surface, unless of course he has progressed to the point where he can recognise and wish to imitate a hatching fly: the nymph fisherman however, and also the wet fly man, are more concerned with aquatic and semi-aquatic insects, since it is mainly the earlier forms in the life cycles of these that they are trying to simulate.

The two more important aquatic orders are the stoneflies and the sedges.

STONEFLIES

The varieties of stoneflies of interest to us comprise the large stonefly, which because of its size is, like the mayfly, in a class of its own, and then, roughly in order of appearance through the year, the February red, early browns, needle flies, yellow sally, small yellow sally and willow fly: this list covers nearly twice as many actual species but often differences between them are too small to be of concern to the angler; in fact after excluding the yellow sallies the only important difference between all of them is that of size. The adult large stoneflies are unmistakable, being at least one-and-a-half inches in length; of the lesser stoneflies the February red, early browns, yellow sally and willow fly are rarely more than half-an-inch and the small yellow sally and the needle flies do not exceed three-eighth inches overall: these are female sizes—the males are always smaller and not much fancied by the fish.

The most immediately noticeable characteristic of the stoneflies, particularly the smaller ones which are of most interest to us, is the difference in apparent size between the flying insect and the same creature at rest. These insects have four wings of which the rear pair are nearly as large as the front ones: when one flies across the water it has the appearance of being as large as a medium sized sedge; however if one is able to mark the place at which it settles one is disconcerted to find a needle-slim insect which the uninitiated will conclude cannot possibly be the creature seen in flight: the deception is brought about not only by the " buzzy " appearance of the insect in flight but by its ability to fold its wings—which in texture are similar to those of a wasp— closely round its already slim body; this applies particularly to the aptly named needle flies which contrive to fold their wings very narrowly, looked at from above, whereas other species tend to look a little flatter from the same aspect.

Stonefly nymphs hatch from the eggs on the bed of the river, and during their growth to maturity tend to crawl rather than swim. They have a superficial resemblance to small earwigs and are readily distinguishable from nymphs of the *Ephemeroptera* by the fact that they have only two, rather stout tails, to the epheme- ropterans' finer three; these tails become much shortened if not actually eliminated in the adult fly. The nymphs of the lesser stoneflies live sub-aqueously for about a year (the large species up to three years), except, curiously, the small yellow sally, which is believed to spend two years as a nymph.

On reaching nymphal maturity, the insect crawls ashore where it splits its skin and emerges as an adult fly, pale-coloured at first but darkening with age. For the next two or three weeks of its life in the winged state, which apart from mating is mainly spent sheltering under leaves or stones, the stonefly is likely to get onto the water only by accident: its main exposure to the fish as a dry fly comes at the end of this period when the female is egg laying, either by scuttering across the water in a general upstream direc- tion or by a regular dipping on to the surface as practised by the small yellow sally; soon after this it dies, usually on the water.

Of the LARGE STONEFLY I confess to little personal experience, having only encountered it on the River Usk; it is of considerable importance in the North of England where, as I mentioned earlier, it is often known as the mayfly. In spite of the fact that it is one of the earliest mentioned flies in angling history a satisfactory artificial pattern does not seem to have evolved, possibly because of the size of the natural.

The most effective means of dealing with a hatch of large stoneflies would seem to be the use of the nymph, or " creeper ", as bait, and this is allegedly deadly—but this is a book on fly fishing! I am not personally too disappointed at the absence of large stoneflies from my own waters; the nymphs (unlike those of the lesser species) are voraciously carnivorous and eat large quantities of the larvae of other insects.

The FEBRUARY RED, also known in some areas as " Old Joan ", appears in its winged state from January through to April so that it comes in for late grayling and early trout at a time when other insect life is scarce. About half-an-inch long when at rest, it has a reddish-brown back but its underside—which the fish see—is distinctly orange; the translucent parts of its wings are a smoky blue but the strong veining in them suffuses the whole wing with its red-brown colour and concentrates itself to give two distinct stripes. There are wet fly patterns aplenty to imitate this fly, of which the Partridge and Orange is one of the best known and is certainly effective, upstream or down; however I know of no " official " dry fly pattern and personally rely on the Dogsbody or Barratt's Bane (or Hereford Alder), and one of these usually does the trick for me.

The EARLY BROWNS are mainly flies of the spring and early summer—say March to June. A little smaller than the February red they are otherwise similar although not so obviously reddish— there is more of a grey tint in their overall brown colour, both wings and body. For artificials the same remarks apply as for the February red, and I cannot do better than suggest the same patterns perhaps scaled down by one hook size, say to 15.

NEEDLE FLIES, otherwise variously known as needle browns or Spanish needles, as a group are the smallest in size of the lesser stoneflies, calling for perhaps size 16 hooks for their artificials; they are about the water through spring, summer and autumn; the spring variety is the smallest and thereafter successive species tend to be a little larger as the year wears on: they are slimmer than

the preceding examples and fold their wings in a narrow inverted
" V " rather than the " U " affected by the other stoneflies; in
colour they are similar to the early browns with a rather more
steely tint to them.

The YELLOW SALLY is to be seen throughout the summer from
April to September; unmistakable because of its colour—yellow
body and paler yellow wings—and about half-an-inch long, dis-
appointingly it is not much favoured by the fish. Happily the reverse is true of the SMALL YELLOW SALLY; this is a different
species entirely although superficially very similar except in size
—it does not exceed three-eights of an inch in length. The small
yellow sally enjoys, regrettably, a shorter winged season than its
larger relative and is essentially an insect of high summer. Once
again there is no formal dry fly pattern that I know of and a con-
sensus of leading authorities leaves one with the impression that
this is a difficult fly to imitate successfully. Fortunately this is not
my experience: for my own dressing I use a 14 hook (or 16 if
conditions demand it) on which I wind a body of yellow unstripped condor herl; there are two hackles, one yellow and one
cream badger, tied together mixed.

The WILLOW FLY, somtimes called " old besom " is a late season
insect and is to be encountered mainly in late August, September
and October : one of the largest of the lesser stoneflies it normally
exceeds half-an-inch in length but not by a great deal; it is an
awkward flier and this often makes it look bigger still, even for a
stonefly; its colour is steel-tinged brown and in this it is very
similar to its earlier cousins. As far as I am aware the only dry fly
specifically designed to imitate the willow fly is the Rev. Edward
Powell's Split Willow. The dressing is as follows : hook : 16;
hackle : very small dark olive; body : stripped peacock quill, dyed
yellow (with picric acid); tail : either dark olive cock hackle-fibres
or a very small tag of palest primrose wool to simulate an egg
cluster. He also specifies wings—thrush primary, rolled, split and
tied spent—though I have not found these necessary but rather that
they made for too much bulk in so small and delicate a fly; an
additional blue-dun hackle is perhaps a better alternative. Apart
from the Split Willow in this instance we do have known patterns
with reputations as specifics for this insect whose effectiveness on
Border water I can confirm : these are the Grey Duster, the Blue
Variant and the Orange Tag. I do not need telling that it is diffi-

cult to imagine three artificial flies quite so different from each other as these, and I am not going even to venture an opinion on why each of these flies, on its day, should be so effective when the willow fly is about.

It will hardly have escaped the reader's notice that although there are a large number of wet fly patterns imitating the lesser stoneflies—most of these of North Country or West of England origin—there appears to be not one named dry fly apart from the Split Willow. There can be little doubt that the reason for this is that this order of insects, of the greatest possible importance on Border waters, is of little consequence on the chalk streams; were the situation otherwise you may be assured that we would have to make a choice between a proliferation of patterns, male and female, nymph adult and spent! To a lesser extent the same might be said of the sedges.

SEDGES

The order *Trichoptera* is probably the largest among aquatic insects, and while many species are of little value from an angling viewpoint on account of smallness or unpalatability or the fact that they are nocturnal, there remains a sufficiently impressive selection to make them of the utmost importance on all types of water, not least on Border fisheries. In spite of the large number of species there are relatively few anglers' names, and while one reason for this is undoubtedly the fact that the order has yet to receive the attention it deserves from angling entomologists, it is nevertheless true that it is possible for a few names to cover the whole sedge spectrum from the angler's standpoint: this is because to a fish a sedge is simply a sedge, and usually desirable; the only variables are likely to be size and colour. The sedge is normally a fussy buzzy insect, in flight not unlike a moth, and if you have the outline right it is only necessary to take all the shades of brown from pale (cinnamon) through to deep chocolate, plus a few shades of grey, and permutate them with small, medium and large, and you are equipped to deal with very nearly every species of sedge that you are likely to encounter: this may be over-simplification, but would certainly meet with most requirements in Border fishing; however you *would* finish up with rather a lot of artificial flies, which is why some rationalisation is necessary.

The life history of the sedges or caddis flies is an enthralling study in its own right, but here we must sketch over it only briefly. After hatching from the eggs on the river bed some of the larvae continue as free-swimming nymphs but the majority make themselves the caddis cases well known to all those interested enough to poke about in shallow places; these may be of sand, small stones, shell, twigs or other vegetable matter and may be cylindrical or tapering, straight or curved, according to species or habitat. Having completed its larval development the insect moults and becomes a pupa, a quiescent state during which the caddis case is anchored to prevent its being washed away, and which can last for days or months depending on species and the time of the year. By the end of pupation the adult insect is fully formed inside the pupal skin; the pupa then leaves the caddis case and swims to the surface using a pair of oar-like legs with which it is conveniently equipped. Arriving at the surface either the pupal skin splits and the adult emerges—which in fast water species is a fairly rapid process— or the pupa swims and drifts until a branch or stone or other projection is encountered and it crawls up it and goes through its metamorphosis at its leisure. As with the stoneflies the newly emerged sedge is pale, but darkens progressively with age unless it is a light variety. Adult life normally lasts about two weeks during which mating and finally egg-laying occur; this is done in a variety of ways, some species swimming and some dipping, while others crawl down into the water—some even to the bed of the stream : death follows soon after and in consequence most females finish up either spent on the water or drowned in it.

From the foregoing it will be seen that the sedges are vulnerable to fish at a number of stages in their life cycle, which normally spans about a year; they are taken as caddis cases in spite of their superb camouflage, and as dry flies and as spent flies : however the stage at which most havoc is wrought is that during which the ripe pupa is swimming to the surface or the safety of the bank and hatching, if it is a surface hatching species; strangely this vital stage is one which has received only desultory attention from the fly dressers, although it is generally accepted that a dry sedge (as opposed to a spent pattern) is often best fished half-drowned, which presupposes its acceptance as a hatching insect.

I referred to a similarity in flight between a sedge and a moth, but this resemblance ends when the insects are at rest; a moth sits with its wings partially spread whereas a sedge holds its wings close to its body, pitched like a roof; nevertheless its wings are opaque, unlike those of the stoneflies and ephemeropterans, being covered by fine hairs. Sedges usually have long—often very long— antennae, but have no tails.

Only two sedges really stand out from the crowd, and I am mentioning them because of this and not because they are necessarily more important as angling flies than any of the other varieties. The first is the great red sedge, sometimes called the bustard in the North of England and famous as the murragh in Ireland where it is dapped. Each of the main aquatic orders seems to have its Goliath and this is the giant among sedges, the female having a wing-span of over two inches; its overall colour is red-brown, the wings having lighter mottling. A mainly nocturnal insect (so that anglers leaving their water before dusk may not be aware of its existence there), its season is from May to September : I know of no formal artificial pattern, wet or dry, probably because like the large stonefly its size is against it and something not dissimilar to a shaving brush is needed; however the fish do appreciate it and the odd outsize pattern may be worth a corner of the fly box.

The other fly is the grannom, a small yellowish-grey sedge (hook size 14), and it earns its mention because of the suddenness and violence of its hatches : one moment there is not a sign, the next the air is filled with what I have heard described as flying chaff; the main trouble is that the hatch will finish as abruptly as it started, while the unprepared angler is still changing his fly! Grannom hatches are localised and unpredictable; they may be unknown to fishermen in one watershed and relatively common to those in the next, but may disappear from there for years at a time : the insects' season is short—only two or three weeks—and very early—late April in the Midlands and Wales but progressively later in the North of England and Scotland. The most successful way of fishing before and during a hatch is likely to be with a wet fly or nymph, since the vast number of naturals on the water make an artificial dry fly somewhat optimistic and the fish are usually more interested in the hatching pupa anyway. Most artificial patterns of the Grannom, wet or dry, are furnished by convention with a green tip to the body if not a body that is wholly green : since this represents the egg-cluster—carried only by the female and then only at the end of her life when she is ovipositing—it seems hardly justified in most patterns, and certainly not in the nymph, wet and spent ones.

For Border fishing it is not strictly necessary to carry specifically dressed dry sedge patterns (though most of us do, of course) because many of our general patterns in the appropriate sizes fill the role admirably; for instance both the Borderer and the Grey Duster stand in for silver sedges; Dogsbody, Wickham's Fancy and Paragon (which is a sedge pattern anyway) cover the shades of brown, and for a very dark sedge there is nothing to beat the Alder.

In due course it will become apparent that I have little time for winged dry flies; some may argue that sedges at least, with their more obtrusive wings, require winged artificials, but I have found this not to be the case; indeed one of the best known artificial sedges of all, Lunn's Caperer, is primarily a hackled pattern. Incidentally this excellent representation of a dark red sedge has been the source of endless confusion and esoteric dispute, since the caperers, particularly in anglers' terms, are cinnamon sedges: this name can only be a chalk stream whimsey.

Most of the above mentioned artificials can also be fished wet, of course, but as I have mentioned earlier it is often better to fish them only half drowned and in this context I would also mention the Invicta, which is generally held to be a useful representation of the hatching sedge. For an upstream nymph pattern when sedges are about it is difficult to better either a Hare's Ear or a Gold-ribbed Hare's Ear.

EPHEMEROPTERA

The average fly fisherman probably knows more—theoretically —about the up-winged flies of the *Ephemeroptera* than those of all the other orders put together; this will be because, as we have already discussed, they are the pre-eminent group of insects on the chalk streams; as such they have been given exhaustive attention by all the great angling authors and by most of the not-so-great as well: they are also of some importance on Border waters, but only relatively, and must yield pride of place to a lot of other insects, notably those of the stonefly and sedge orders already discussed.

The order includes such famous names as march brown, olive,

blue-winged olive, iron blue, pale watery and of course the mayfly, which is the giant of the order, being very much larger than most of the others. The average life cycle is about a year (although the mayfly takes about two years to reach maturity) and begins as with most aquatic insects with the nymph hatching from the egg, either on the stream bed or attached to some under-surface feature; thereafter the nymphs of different species vary in their way of life: mayfly nymphs burrow into silt; some like the blue-winged olive find themselves thick weed growth to live among and such nymphs as the march brown, which live in the swiftest currents, are able as a result of their specialised shape to maintain their position on smooth stones to which they are able to cling like limpets. It will readily be seen that because of the characteristics I have described these three types of nymph are not much help to the nymph fisherman for most of their lives—not in fact until they are ready to swim to the surface in order to become adult flies: it is with the fourth type that his main interest will lie and which he will try to copy with his artificials; these are the nymphs of such species as the various olives, pale wateries and iron blue which are freeswimming and therefore available to the fish for most of the time. It may be thought that because of their diverse requirements in the way of habitat the various types I have mentioned will not be found together in the same stretch of water, but this is not so; the liveliest of streams can have its silted backwaters and its small beds of weed just outside the main current, so that it is normal to expect an assortment of species in most Border waters. Most freeswimming ephemeropteran nymphs are of a conventional shape, varying only in size and colour; they have a torpedo-like outline but the abdomen—occupying the rear two-thirds of their length— is usually slim and tapering whereas the thorax, which carries the three pairs of legs, is bulkier and somewhat hump-backed where the wings are developing; the thorax is normally darker in colour than the abdomen which is often fringed with delicate gill filaments; all these nymphs have three short tails (regardless of whether the adult fly has three or two) which are furnished with dense fine hairs to make an efficient swimming aid.

On completion of its nymphal development the insect undergoes its transformation into its winged state; mostly this is done by its swimming to the surface and climbing out of its split skin, though some species emerge from the nymphal shuck under water and complete the journey in a bubble of gas, while others crawl ashore: it is the first of these variations which is of most concern to the angler, for the fish are often more keen to take the ascending nymph or the hatching fly in its moment of vulnerability than the dun itself. Duns of fastwater species like the march brown will often hatch and leave the water almost simultaneously unless they happen to come up in a patch of calm water; others, fortunately for the angler, will rest for a few moments on the water to dry and strengthen their wings before lumbering off in search of sanctuary. " Lumbering " is an apposite description of the flight of the dun; it still has another moult to undergo before reaching adulthood and so is still carrying some weight; for this reason its flight is also characterised by a somewhat drooping abdomen. Having found shelter under a leaf near the waterside the dun will rest there for maybe twenty-four hours, though this pause can be longer in cold or wet weather conditions; then the final moult takes place and the insect steps right out of its skin, wings, eyes, tails and all, and is now (in anglers' terms) a spinner. Once the two adult stages have been seen there is little possibility, even at a distance, of confusing one with the other: the dun, being covered in microscopic water-repellent hairs is dull and sober hued; its wings though translucent are not transparent; in contrast the spinner is sparkling, its colours often jewel-like and its wings gauzy; the flight of the dun is fluttery, laboured and tail-heavy whereas that of the spinner is dancing and vital, and while the tails of the dun are a little longer than its body those of the spinner are half as long again.

The spinners now take to the air and the males of each species gather into hovering swarms to await the advent of females of their kind; as soon as the female approaches the swarm several males may detach themselves and the first one there will mate with her in flight, and return to the swarm. The position of these swarms relative to the water and other features, and the pattern of flight of the males in a swarm, differ between species; it is possible therefore, if these patterns are studied, for an angler to identify the spinner soon to be on the water without actually examining an individual.

After mating the female may return to shelter for a while or she may proceed immediately to egg-laying: this once more is done in a variety of ways by different species; the dipping method is practised by some, often to the extent of settling momentarily on the water; others release their eggs above the water like minia-ture bombs; others again will crawl down into the water to attach their eggs to suitable supports such as stones, and this is the method used by some of those species I have already mentioned as having free-swimming nymphs, namely the various olives and the iron blue. These spinners, being now spent will drift up towards the surface, and if not already drowned will be too far gone to be able to re-penetrate the surface film (in theory the insects' water-repellent characteristics should enable them to return to the top-side of the surface in a fairly dry state, and this indeed happens on still or smooth-running water; however the normal turbulence of a Border stream will usually drown them before the surface is reached); they are likely therefore to continue downstream just under the surface, and this will often account for the phenomenon when there is seen to be a good rise of fish but no discernible fly on the water.

Those females who do their egg-laying from above the surface will go on going through the motions after their eggs are ex-pended, until finally they fall exhausted—" spent "—on the water (but are joined there by only a few of the males) and are carried away in the surface film.

The MAYFLY, otherwise the greendrake (the dun), the greydrake (female spinner before egglaying), the blackdrake (male spinner) and the spent gnat (spent spinner) is probably the best known of all anglers' insects; the name covers three very similar species. As with many aquatic insects the females are noticeably larger than the males, their bodies being nearly an inch in length in the mature nymph and dun stages and slightly smaller in the spinner. The female dun has slightly mottled olive wings, dark olive legs, a dark brown thorax, and abdomen of a fawn colour with darker markings along the back; the female spinner has bluish transparent wings with faint mottling, dark grey legs, black thorax and an abdomen translucent and almost white except for the tip which is brown; the males are darker and, as mentioned, smaller; this in-sect has three tails.

Contrary to the expectation implied by its name the mayfly's season is usually about the first two weeks of June: I feel that this may be due to some tinkering about with the calendar which went on in the eighteenth century. One often hears mayfly time described as " duffers' fortnight ", but this is far from my experience on Border waters, for fish are no easier to catch then than at any other time: the main difference is that it does provide the angler with an opportunity of coming to terms with better fish than he will see during the rest of the season; the hoary cannibal to whom normal size flies are just not worth the trouble, may well decide that the bigger mouthful provided by the mayfly will justify the effort.

Presumably because of a need to work up pressure inside its skin in order to hatch, the unfortunate nymph is compelled to wait about near the surface for a considerable period—up to twenty minutes has been noted (though not on Border waters)—before it makes the breakthrough; at this stage it is clearly at the mercy of the fish, who usually make the most of their opportunity, and I find it strange therefore that little is heard of Mayfly Nymph patterns, and even wet flies seem little used these days.

For the first few days of the mayfly Border fish are very wary of the natural—presumably being apprehensive of its size—and a full sized conventional dry fly can be relied on to put fish down; at this time I find either the Alder or the Dogsbody effective, and wait until the fish are well on the naturals before attempting a Mayfly proper. Artificial Mayfly patterns are legion and rarely consistent in their attraction; a fly which takes fish well one day can fail miserably the next. For my part I normally use a reversed fore-and-aft hackled pattern based on an idea of David Jacques, which I will describe later, and if this lets me down I revert to my normal Border artificials in the larger sizes.

There are many fishermen who carry on through mayfly time with their normal flies, not bothering with formal Mayfly imitations, and enjoy as much success—often more—as those who try to imitate; a Grey Duster in size 10 or 12 is a fair representation of a spent gnat and can usually be depended upon to kill well throughout the mayfly season. Fortunately fish prefer their Mayfly artificials to be rather smaller than the natural, and I have found it a grave mistake not to accommodate them in this respect.

Among the normal sized ephemeropterans the most widespread and commonly encountered come under the general label of OLIVES; this term covers an assortment of species within the same genus (apart from the blue-winged olive) all of whom have two tails in the adult, whose nymphs are free-swimming and whose

females lay their eggs under the water, and whose principal difference from each other from an angler's standpoint is in size and
season.

The LARGE DARK OLIVE (spring olive, blue dun) has a body
about three-eighths of an inch in length and is primarily a cold
weather species, being mostly in evidence during February and
March and also in September and October, and indeed throughout
the winter: the SMALL DARK OLIVE has a body length of not more
than a quarter of an inch and is about the water from February to
November, while the MEDIUM OLIVE falls between the two former
in size (though the " medium " refers to colour) and is to be seen
from March to September. The general colouring of the olive duns
is a dull olive-grey, although the medium and small are more olive
than the dark, and the small is relatively the palest of the three
(why it is called the small *dark* olive escapes me, especially since
it is also known as a pale watery); all have black tipped legs. The
spinners have transparent colourless wings, almost black thoraces
and rich red-brown bodies becoming translucent when spent—
the well-known red spinners.

There is no shortage of artificial patterns from which to choose,
but perhaps the most exact imitation of the duns is the Greenwell's Glory; a fellow angler once told me that he had seen " a
splendid hatch of Greenwell's " and it wasn't until later that I
remembered to be amused, so clear a picture did his description
convey! I mostly use my own version of the Rough Olive but
another dun pattern which I find effective on Border streams is
Kite's Imperial, while for the red spinner there is little to beat the
Pheasant Tail.

The IRON BLUE belongs to the same genus as the olives and like
them has a free-swimming nymph and the characteristic of sub-
aqueous ovipositing; it is a very different colour, however, the
dun being a very dark blue-grey, almost black in some light; it is
a very small insect, fractionally larger than the small dark olive,
with a body length of about a quarter of an inch; nevertheless the
iron blue is a great favourite of the fish who will often ignore all
other species when it is about. The season of the iron blue is from
April to November, but it is most in evidence from May to September; while it is therefore clearly a summer fly it has no association with hot weather and can be more confidently looked for on
those days, particularly in May, when the weather is unseasonably

cold and blustery. The male spinners of the iron blue tend to get on the water more frequently than those of other species, and if they do they are well liked by the fish and a problem arises which calls for acute observation, especially if the light is fading. Remember that the female spinner may be *under* the surface, in which case a tiny *drowned* Pheasant Tail should meet the need; however the male spinner has a white body, and if the fish are showing a preference for him a small Grey Duster in the surface film may prove to be the answer.

The BLUE-WINGED OLIVE is not a member of the olives already discussed and its name can therefore give rise to some confusion; it is among the few ephemeropterans who carry all three nymphal tails into adulthood and is altogether a more colourful fly than the rather sober olives. Roughly similar in size to the large dark olive, and therefore rather smaller than the march brown, the blue-winged olive's season is from June to October; in the warm days of July and August it inclines to hatch in the late evening, but earlier and later in the year it is to be seen about all day. The blue-winged olive dun is characterised by its relatively large slate-coloured wings : otherwise, having described it as more colourful than the olives it is difficult to be specific about its colouring, since it is subject to much variation, from bright olive-green to yellow-green, possibly as a result of ageing; there is often a bit of red-brown about it also, usually towards the tail. The female spinner (the sherry spinner) is even more prone to colour variation; her thorax is a dark golden-brown but her abdomen starts its spinner life with a distinct green colour, possibly borrowed from the egg-mass inside, and as this is extruded the abdomen becomes yellower but by the time the fly is spent this will often have turned to golden red. Prior to ovipositing the female extrudes all her eggs while flying hoveringly upstream; she supports the egg-mass by curling the end of her abdomen under her like a fish-hook and in this attitude is one of the most easily recognised of aquatic insects; when the extrusion is complete she will locate an area of fast water and dip into it, freeing the eggs into the current.

The blue-winged olive has clearly presented considerable difficulty to generations of chalk stream fly designers, but fortunately for Border fishermen our fish are less critical and I have found both the Imperial and the Dogsbody successful. The sherry spinner is more of a problem since the ubiquitous Pheasant Tail is perhaps a little too dark in the body, but it is usually possible to find a strand which is more golden in colour, and this will often suffice.

PALE WATERY is a generic term applied to five different up-winged flies, three of which are of interest to Border fishermen; one of these—the small dark olive—we have already dealt with; the remaining two are nowadays designated the greater and lesser SPURWINGS, presumably from a tiny projection located on the already small rear wings which you need a magnifying glass to see. The greater spurwing is known to me as the blue-winged pale watery, whose season is from July to September; its wings are similar in colour to those of the blue-winged olive and its body is paler than those of the olives; in size it is similar to the medium olive. The lesser spurwing is the little sky blue, a tiny fly like the small dark olive but paler; its season is from April to October, but from June to August it tends to be a dusk hatching fly. From a Border fishing point of view the same artificials as are used for the olives and the blue-winged olive, in appropriate sizes, will cope with the spurwings.

Among Border ephemeropterans the MARCH BROWN, I fancy, is an insect more heard of than seen, for it inclines to be local in distribution and more at home on the bigger fast rivers such as the Usk in Wales and the Tweed in Scotland. Somewhat larger than the large dark olive, where it occurs the march brown is likely to put in a swift, prolific and soon-over appearance whenever there is a bit of sunshine between noon and teatime in late March and April. An altogether browner fly than those already described, the dun has fawn coloured wings covered in dark brown veining except for a clear patch near the middle of each, an olive-brown body, and two tails. Because of the disinclination of the dun to hang about on the water once hatched, the nymph and wet fly are the more important artificials; the Silver March Brown, I believe, owes its success to the fact that its body material imitates effectively the layer of air under the skin which the insect produces or ingests in order to build up the pressure required to split the skin. However the dry March Brown makes an excellent sedge pattern on all waters.

The march brown spinner is of little interest either to the fish or the fisherman, unlike that of the LATE MARCH BROWN which is known as the great red spinner and is a different species alto-gether; paradoxically the nymph and dun of the late march brown are themselves of little concern to the angler, since the nymph is bottom-clinging and crawls out of the water to hatch. This is a large insect, the female approaching the mayfly in size but with march brown colouring.

The march brown has a close relative, less publicised and quite unlike it (although the nymphs are indistinguishable), which is more familiar to anglers on smaller run-of-the-mill Border waters; this is the YELLOW UPRIGHT, though where it got its name from I have no idea, for it is no more upright or yellower than most other upwinged flies: if anything the dun is more like a smaller edition of the blue-winged olive only with a broader, flatter body and only two tails, and the same artificials will do. For the interested angler-naturalist the give-away is a tiny triangular mark on the top-side of each thigh joint, which can just be seen by the naked eye in a good light, and which confirms its relationship to its more famous cousin. I mention the fly specifically because of its spinner, whose male mating swarm is one of the commonest sights on Border waters in late spring and early summer; this is not necessarily, I think, because the fly is any more prolific than others mentioned, but because its males swarm lower and closer to the river and so capture the anglers' attention more readily. This spinner has a toffee-coloured thorax, a flattish red-brown body getting browner towards the tail, straw-coloured legs and the fish don't like it much: my reason for describing it is that in doing so I may avert disappointment in a beginner who, seeing the swarm, concludes that all he has to do is wait for the spinners to fall in order to enjoy a spanking rise!

NOTABLE INDIVIDUAL FLIES

I have one more truly aquatic insect to deal with, but it belongs not to any of the three orders that we have already covered but to the great order *Diptera* (two-winged) which also gives us the bluebottles, wasps, cowdung flies and countless other terrestrial insects. I am referring to the BLACK GNAT, and before avid readers of the classics of angling entomology start claiming that the black gnat is not an aquatic but a terrestrial fly, let me say that I have read those books too; they tell us that the black gnat is called *bibio johannis* because it appears on St. John's day (and that its larger relative the hawthorn fly appears on St. Mark's day), but they do not tell us what on earth the tiny insect is which the fish are taking so eagerly from late April onward—St. John's day being also Midsummer Day. Now I do not wish to detract from the importance of *bibio johannis* (or of his larger cousin the hawthorn fly—St. Mark's day is April 25th) because the fish will take these insects keenly *when* they get on the water; but being terrestrial flies they will be available to the fish no more and no less frequently than all the other terrestrial insects of the waterside who get on the water by accident. The popularity attaching to the black gnat with both the fish and the fisherman is such as can only possibly derive from an aquatic insect which is on or in the water regularly, and I have no reservation in saying that the real black gnat (as opposed to the " true " black gnat) is the reed smut. What angler has not often seen the cloud of myriads of frantically gyrating tiny flies poised just above the surface of the water? So fast is their movement within the whirling cloud that it seems to be defying the laws of motion by not itself moving to any appreciable degree. These then are reed smuts, or as I shall call them from now on, black gnats. There is a close superficial resemblance between the reed smut and *bibio johannis*—both after all belong to the same order and have the general appearance of a tiny housefly—: however the housefly has a thorax and abdomen of approximately equal thickness, whereas the black gnat has a relatively large thorax and slim abdomen, giving it a hunched appearance from which no doubt stems the American name for it of buffalo gnat. Distantly related to the chironomids—the midges and buzzers of the reservoir fisherman—there are a large number of species of black gnats only some of which occur in any one place at any one time, since the species vary according to the speed of the current and the hardness of the water; however, provided they are large enough to be imitated (they vary from the minute to a maximum length of about a quarter of an inch) they can all be treated as one for angling purposes.

The life cycle of the black gnat is very similar to those of most other truly aquatic insects: only to be found in running water, the larva hatches sub-aqueously from the egg and during its underwater life is dirty-cream in colour and resembles in shape a miniature Indian club, the head being at the handle end. The larva extrudes a thread wherever it goes for safety purposes, and in company with a number of its fellows will criss-cross a stone or leaf with a net of these filaments; this net provides a *pied-à-terre* for the members of the colony, each of whom is equipped with minute hooks on its nether end by which it remains anchored to the net, leaving it free to feed in the passing current; locomotion is achieved by jack-knifing in the manner of an acrobatic tumbler, using alternately the hooks in the tail and a similar set on the head. Black gnat larvae on their safety nets are of course available to browsing fish, though not in a way that is helpful to the fisherman; however when alarmed the larvae will often swing into the current on the end of their threads, and since as often as not the reason for their alarm will be a feeding fish the situation has distinct possibilities. It is likely that this habit in the black gnat larvae, which is also found in the larvae of certain sedge flies, accounts for the frequent success of a wet fly or nymph held stationary downstream.

The insect pupates by spinning itself a cocoon which it attaches to a weed stem, underwater twig or similar suitable anchorage: on completion of pupation the adult fly splits its pupal skin, emerges from its cocoon and rides to the surface in a bubble of gas which projects it dry into the open air. The swarms mentioned earlier are no doubt for the purpose of mating, and from time to time a mated pair so far forget themselves as to fall onto the surface of the water, and here we have the knotted midge. Egg-laying by most of the species is done by the female crawling down under the water and then becoming spent, like the olives and iron blue of the *Ephemeroptera,* and usually engenders a similar response from the fish.

Various artificial patterns of Black Gnats are well known: The Knotted Midge I have already mentioned and this is one of the most effective Border patterns, as I have no doubt it is elsewhere; clearly one has a better chance of imitating two such tiny insects on a single hook than only one. For some reason which I have never been able to explain or have explained to me, a small Dogsbody, which looks nothing like a black gnat, must be regarded as a specific when the fish are taking the black gnat.

Any surprise which may have been occasioned by my allotting to the black gnat the status of aquatic insect may now be eclipsed by my intention of assigning a similar dignity to the DADDY LONG-LEGS or crane fly. Nevertheless there are in fact 290-odd species of this insect, of which those whose larvae—the leatherjackets—

are anathema to the tenders of lawns and golf courses are very much in the minority to those whose preference is for a life by the waterside: many species, including the largest, are creatures of marshy places, others are semi-aquatic while some are truly aquatic, their larvae among the stones of the riverbed being not dissimilar to the leatherjacket of the bowling green.

Crane flies are about throughout the summer but sometimes achieve plague proportions in late July and August, and when there are a lot of them about near the water a goodly proportion finish up on it, for like the alder they are poor fliers and at the mercy of a temperamental breeze. The fish like them but are chary of odd specimens, no doubt—as is the case with precocious may-flies—on account of their size, if it is some time since they saw one previously; but when there are sufficient daddys about for the fish to become accustomed to them the response can be as good as in a good mayfly hatch. Although this is a seasonal thing it is well worthwhile having the old artificial in the box; Leonard West and T. J. Hanna each designed one and I will give my own dressing later on.

The ALDER is a semi-aquatic insect, which is to say that part of its life cycle only is aquatic and the remainder terrestrial: an ubiquitous insect in its season of May and June, it also enjoys a high personal popularity with most fishermen, many of whom comment happily on seeing the first alder of the season in the same way as others welcome the first cuckoo. The artificial also is one of the most popular; few of us are without it and it is usually among the first flies that a beginner is advised to buy. All of which is rather odd, since there is no doubt that the fish are not at all partial to alder diet and are apt rather pointedly to ignore the natural fly: this is of course not a purely personal opinion for it is a recurrent theme in much fly fishing literature and is confirmed by the vast majority of anglers with whom I have discussed it, and one rarely hears of an alder turning up in an authenticated autopsy. My own conviction was crystallised some years ago when I was fishing a Worcestershire stream during the alder season when quite a number of alders were being deposited on the water by a gusty cross-wind: I had found a feeding fish rising intermittently to surface fly and filling in the time between by nymphing; while I watched, several alders floated over him only to be ignored, although he was rising between them to take something which I was not able to identify. After a while I cast to him, without a great deal of hope, for the fly I had on was a dry Alder; but he rose to it at once and took without a moment's hesitation. Had that fish been of takeable size I would have been able to round off the tale by revealing what he had been feeding on, but the fact remains that after almost ostentatiously ignoring a number of natural alders he accepted an artificial one with complete confidence.

I have seen the natural alder described as having the body of a dark medium sedge and the wings of a stonefly; this is not strictly accurate because it folds its wing in much the same way as a sedge —tentwise—although their texture has a similarity to that of a stonefly's. The veining of an alder's wings is, like the stonefly's, strong and dark, although the translucent membrane between the veins, brownish in a stonefly, is slightly tinged with red in the alder as is its abdomen, which no doubt accounts for the magenta-dyed peacock herl in Charles Kingsley's original pattern: the hump-backed thorax is nearly black.

The alder larva lives underwater until it is ready to pupate: it is an ugly brown creature with a broad head and thorax and a sharply tapering abdomen which is fringed with gill filaments, but it is prolific and free swimming and thus of much importance as a nymph, for plenty of alder larvae *are* found in autopsies. The larva leaves the water to pupate in the bankside soil, so that the adult insect emerges from a hole in the ground and has little to do with the water until ready for egg-laying; even then the female does it on land, but deposits her eggs on vegetation that is close enough to the water to ensure that the larvae do not have far to walk, and they make straight for the water after hatching.

Although the adult natural alder is manifestly not popular with the fish, it is not really difficult to account for the popularity of the artificial fly, particularly on Border streams: after all something which imitates a cross between a sedge and a stonefly can hardly fail! The artificial Alder is one of the few dry flies whose wings I approve of—one cannot, after all, argue against success; its general make-up, however, is in line with the basic design, indefinitely permutated, which characterises successful Border flies; among its near relatives the Coch-y-bonddhu, John Storey, Treacle Parkin and Coachman spring to mind at once as killing flies, and there is no doubt that these flies represent all things to all fish—

that they are seen as sedges, stoneflies, beetles, bluebottles and all manner of adventitious terrestrial insects—and are successful when what they look like to the fish coincides with what the fish fancy to eat.

Now that we have started to discuss terrestrial insects this may be as good a point as any to mention the FLYING ANT: all ants except workers start life with wings to enable them to swarm, which they normally do in late summer. When such a swarm on the move to new premises happens to cross a river, for some reason large numbers manage to fall in, and the effect can be electrifying; if an angler is lucky this phenomenon may happen to him once in his fishing life; if he is without a suitable artificial pattern, red or black, he is likely to remain permanently embittered.

Few anglers give even a passing thought to the GREENFLY, and if they do it is likely to be in the context of horticulture rather than angling; yet they should take note that there is probably a much larger population of these small aphids beside their river than is to be found in all their collective rose gardens; further that fish adore greenfly and that on many Borders waters they form the staple diet of the fish for long periods at a time. The favourite wild habitat of greenfly is nettles, and where there are extensive nettle beds adjoining or overhanging the water a continuous trickle of the insects may be assumed to be entering the current during most of the temperate months, increasing in proportion to the gustiness of the wind. Since a greenfly reaches maturity in only two weeks from birth and the output of progeny from one female is astronomical, a steady supply is assured. What is the use, you may say, of all this when to imitate a greenfly would require a hook size 22 or even 24? I have another small tale to tell.

I was fishing a Border stream in the July of a long hot summer when the water was already desperately low and completely clear: " fishing " is something of a misnomer; I was working disconsolately upstream seeing fish after fish take off long before I was anywhere near casting distance, and had almost reached the point of giving it up as hopeless. At the top of a gravelly stickle up which I was working was a slow, shallow pool with the main glide running along one side; as my eyes reached the level of the surface of the pool I became conscious of what at first I thought was the end of a sunken branch agitating the water just above the point where the main glide of the pool spilled onto the stickle; a second look told me that what in fact I was seeing were the dorsal and caudal fins of a good trout which was feeding feverishly with most of his back out of the water. It was a nice problem: whatever I was going to offer him must be placed not more than an inch or so upstream of his nose otherwise drag would set in while it was in his vision; thus he had to be offered something which he was prepared to accept without a moment's hesitation. To minimise the drag I crept to a point from which I could cast to him from a fairly wide angle, and proceeded to offer him almost everything I had of a suitable size, but all I got out of it was the satisfaction of not having put him down—though I think his preoccupation with his dinner was mainly responsible for that—; I tried him with a small nymph—usually a certainty for a visibly feeding fish—but I don't think he even saw it since his eyeballs must have been almost in the surface film. Then from the recesses of my mind came the recollection of something I had read about similar circumstances—by Courtney Williams—and naming the Ermine Moth; now this fly is a standard Border pattern invented by that eminent designer of Border flies the Rev. Edward Powell, but is usually reserved for use in the late evening when its light colouring shows up well and the pale spotted moths which it represents are about the water; its general appearance (grey partridge hackles, white rabbit's fur body ribbed with black, and yellow-orange tag) is evocative of a liquorice allsort and it certainly seemed incongruous in the present circumstances. Nevertheless I decided to give it a try; I had a small one with me and I made it look even smaller by clipping the hackle, and I did not treat it with flotant. Not to make a long story out of it the fish pounced on the fly at the first offer, and I was so grateful to him that I released him at once, sizeable though he was. I then went to where he had been lying to try and discover what he had been feeding on, and at first could detect nothing although I got right down to water level; however I had with me the business end of a child's tiddler-net—a useful accessory for catching insects in—and held it in the water letting the current sieve through it. The answer was, of course, greenfly, but what useful lessons had been learned: firstly that greenfly can be coming down in quantity and yet so imbedded in the surface film as not to be visible above water, and in this joining the spinners of olives, iron blue and black gnats in being the possible cause of rises to invisible insects —often dimissed as " smutting "—; then the efficacy of the Ermine Moth in such circumstances, an asset which I am now aware was well-known to its inventor. My Ermine Moth got me two more fish that afternoon and many, many more since, under similar circumstances.

Of the remaining land-based insects of the Border waterside which regularly find their way onto the water, most can be accounted for with one or other of the general Border patterns, many of which I have already mentioned. Even so many have their own special patterns, including the bluebottle, oakfly, haw-thorn fly, cowdung and the coch-y-bonddhu to name but a few of the more popular. Reference to the coch-y-bonddhu leads me to a comment on beetles in general; this particular insect does not occur, I am sorry to say, on my own regular waters, though it has given me sport enough in North Wales and its artificial is a kill-ing fly wherever Border fishing is practised. However beetles of other species not only get onto the water far more frequently than most anglers realise but are relished by the fish, and it is a rare autopsy which does not reveal the odd one or two. Most beetles can fly, although they generally need a moment or two of pre-paration—in order to arrange their wing-cases—before they can do so; in consequence when they start to fall they do not have time to save themselves, unlike other winged insects; further when they are flying their range is uncertain, due to their weight, and as a result an involuntary touch-down on the water is com-mon. Here I have referred to mainly terrestrial beetles, but it should be remembered also that there is an immense and varied population of aquatic beetles whose whole life cycle is perpetu-ated in or near the water; probably the best known of these is the corixa or lesser water boatman, although this is mainly a slow- or still-water insect.

Beetles in general have received scant attention from the fly designers so that in consequence there are few named patterns, a Palmer fly (seal's fur body, hackled all the way down and ribbed with gold wire or tinsel) in the appropriate colour is probably the best dry representation, so that a Black Palmer would be a suitable pattern for the black or very dark beetles which are in the majority—although any artificial fly which has a peacock herl body (such as those named in connexion with the alder) has an odds-on chance of being taken for a beetle.

The terrestrial beetle which in its season is possibly of most specific interest to Border fishermen is the BLACK-TIPPED SOLDIER BEETLE: soldier and sailor beetles are handled rather vaguely in most angling literature perhaps because the terms cover a number of species. Oddly enough the black-tipped is not closely related to the others; it is a medium-sized elongated beetle of a general bright orange colour, the orange of the wing cases being somewhat darker than the rest and shading almost to black at their tips; it flies freely and appears in profusion in the waterside meadows during the summer, showing a preference for umbelliferous vegetation such as hemlock and cow-parsnip; a gust of wind can put hundreds of them on the water where they are welcomed by the fish, possibly because they are a " soft-shelled " beetle. The recognised dry imitations for the soldier beetles are either the Red Palmer or the Soldier Palmer, but on Border waters at any rate I find the Welsh Fusilier by far the more effective.

Because it is a crustacean and not an insect (although the two classes are closely related) the FRESHWATER SHRIMP tends to get left out in the cold in works of angling entomology; also of course, chalk stream practice has tended to frown on the imitation of anything which does not actually appear above the surface of the water at some stage in its life cycle. Nevertheless the shrimp is of considerable importance in Border fishing since the fish seem to prefer it to any other single food animal. They are seldom absent from the stomach contents of trout and it is not uncommon for an aldermanic grayling to be seen browsing systematically over a gravelly bottom, nudging aside each stone in turn and grabbing the fleeing shrimps, his progress marked by small puffs of displaced silt; that such grayling are indeed feeding on shrimp is often not too difficult to prove for when a grayling can be found doing this it is usually possible to catch him more easily than at most other times.

While fairly ubiquitous in their distribution, freshwater shrimps have two minimal requirements—oxygen and calcium—and although Border streams provide the former in plenty there are some which are too acid or peaty to sustain shrimp life; for the same reason the degree of calcium content in a water will determine the maximum size to which shrimps will grow in that water, and it follows that the shrimps of a normal Border stream will be substantially smaller than their relatives in a chalk stream, and will rarely be longer than half-an-inch overall. During the early summer shrimps change in colour from their normal olivey-brown to a mating livery of bright orange, and thereby become doubly desirable to the fish; at this time a small Partridge and Orange Spider is most effective and indeed most orange bodied wet flies will tempt fish. To meet this particular requirement I evolved a mating shrimp pattern which I called the Amorous Shrimp; the dreadful implied pun will fortunately only be obvious esoterically to those interested in the contemporary theatre, and to them I apologise. I will give the details of the dressing later.

At first sight the freshwater shrimp appears to be an extremely simple animal to imitate effectively in an artificial fly; its curved back seems closely to follow the outline of the bend of the hook, and since all its appendages in the way of legs, feelers and tail lie in a downward direction, it seems the obvious thing to do to start with a palmer-tied fly and to give it a shell-back of plastic or similar material which will have the effect of forcing all the hackle fibres downward. By dressing it in this way it is possible to produce a most exact and lifelike imitation, and of course several such patterns do exist. However what is not taken into account is the fact that a shrimp has to do most of its swimming more or less upside-down because of the keel-weighting effect of its shell-back, and even when feeding, or otherwise conducting itself when not actually travelling, it rarely assumes the attitude which to us would be the right way up. It follows that the shell-backed artificial can only be representative of the shrimp at those times when it is least practicable to imitate it, and it would seem that the most expedient way of " backing it both ways " would be to use a palmer-tied fly *without* the shell-back, so that the fish can have it whichever way they like.

At best an incompetent swimmer, the shrimp is likely to be found doing it voluntarily only in the slackest currents; at other times it will stay in the protection of stones and its progress will be by crawling, mainly on its side; nevertheless it can be found in quantity in the swiftest places, although any which are loose in the current will normally have been involuntarily displaced.

Chapter Four

SOME THOUGHTS ON CASTING

SOME FISHERMEN have fathers or uncles or elder brothers who are themselves anglers, and from whom they were able to learn their skills at first hand and probably at an early age. It is probable that most of these do not realise how fortunate they are, for not only will they have their entire lives from boyhood onward during which to enjoy their sport, but they will have had the inestimable benefit of personal demonstration and tutorage. In this I can speak from the heart, for I was not one of this happy band: I was first bitten by the fishing bug comparatively late in life and in addition, due to my circumstances at the time, I knew almost nobody who could be of any help to me. In consequence I learned my basic fly fishing, including my fly dressing, from books, and remember well my efforts to master the art of casting in a field with my rod in one hand and a book in the other.

Nowadays expert casting tuition is widely available and for the most part at a modest fee, and fly dressing is taught by experts at winter evening classes throughout the country, so that my first advice to any beginner would be to take advantage of this. For Border fishing care should be taken in choosing a casting instructor whose main concern is not with reservoir casting; for this comparatively new extension of the sport, new techniques have arisen which are quite inimical to Border fishing and which should be kept quite separate from it.

Casting can of course be learned from a friend who is himself a competent caster, but competence in an activity does not in any way imply a competence to teach it, and it is as possible to acquire bad habits in casting as it is in driving a motor car as a result of learning from an unqualified instructor.

An acquaintance of mine who teaches casting claims that he can have *anyone* casting a reasonable line in twenty minutes, and casting well in an hour: he then sends them away to get in some practice under field conditions and suggests that they return in due course for a further short lesson during which he can check faults. How painless this appears compared to my own apprenticeship only someone else who has done it the hard way could appreciate. At the first opportunity I did myself go to a professional for critical instruction, although by that time I regarded myself as fairly competent, and was thus able to correct some incipient bad habits of my own; this course of action I can also recommend to others similarly placed.

In thus strongly advocating personal instruction I do not wish to detract in any way from some of the excellent books which exist both on casting and fly dressing, or suggest that they should not be read. But I do feel that their main benefit is to be used in conjunction with first hand tuition rather than as a substitute for it.

I think that it can now be taken for granted that it is not my intention to try and teach my readers how to cast; in fact I am assuming that they can already do so, but that they may nevertheless derive some benefit from what I have to say on points of technique in the context of Border fishing.

I will not, I hope, be labelled as reactionary if I say that I am sure, as far as my own fishing is concerned, that the old ways are the best: I am thinking especially of two casting precepts which seem to have gone overboard in recent years mainly as a result of the increasing popularity of reservoir fly fishing, namely that (first) the rod butt on the back cast should not move appreciably beyond the 12 o'clock position, and secondly that the elbow of the casting arm should remain close to the side.

Bearing in mind that we are discussing what is in itself a specialised branch of the sport, I would say that compliance with both of these old rules is essential to successful casting on the type of waters with which we are concerned. Much of our casting will be done from a kneeling or even a sitting position and we almost never have the whole of the sky for our back cast: the analogy between the back cast and the setting of a spring has been used often enough, but you cannot set this particular spring until the rod tip has passed sufficiently far beyond the point at which the butt has been checked to "wind it up" to its maximum efficiency; if this checking point is substantially to the rear of the vertical, the line will probably sag before it can straighten and must hit the ground if not something worse. My own feeling is that if you cannot develop sufficient power in your back cast by the time the rod butt reaches the vertical you are unlikely to acquire any more by letting it go back a bit further. In this connexion the use of the word "vertical" is perhaps misconceived, since opportunities for performing an overhead cast are not frequent in Border fishing; much more common is the side cast, but since this is basically an overhead cast carried out in a roughly horizontal plane the same rules apply: perhaps we should stick to "12 o'clock" rather than "vertical".

As to the growing recourse to casting at arm's length, there can be no justification for it in Border fishing and I have yet to be convinced that it is sound practice anywhere else: if the object is to obtain greater distance by starting with greater height it would seem to me simpler to acquire a rod a couple of feet longer and to continue to cast properly, and let the rod do the work it is supposed to, instead of one's unfortunate shoulder. One hardly needs to be a student of ergonomics to appreciate that casting at arm's length must be inefficient and, more important, inaccurate. When I taught myself to cast I followed the traditional advice by imagining that I held some slim object between my elbow and my side, in fact for some time I actually did hold such an object there; now the habit is ingrained and I commend it. Apart from the fact that in the confined spaces usually to be encountered in Border fishing one needs to organise oneself into as compact a casting unit as possible, elbow-by-the-side delivery is infinitely more accurate and controlled, and when power *is* required it has not only the shoulder but the whole body behind it.

It will perhaps be not inopportune here to remind the reader, since the word "power" has been mentioned, that the main effort in the cast should be in the back cast—the setting of the spring—and that in the forward cast considerations of accuracy, control and delicate presentation should be uppermost. With regard to the last mentioned I have found that one of the best ways of achieving the required delicacy, especially with a dry fly, is to follow the old adage about aiming about a foot above the water and letting the fly drift down onto it.

THE NEED TO CAST A LOOSE LINE, AND THE FOLLOW THROUGH

Another important aid in the accomplishment of delicate presentation is the follow-through. The significance of this in most sports involving the movement of an implement such as a golf club or even a long bow is well known, although many anglers do not realise that it applies to them also. In casting, the follow-through is produced by " following the fly down " with the rod tip, at the same time moving the rod towards the fly (the elbow can leave the side now!), and allowing the body to lean forward.

Someone who knew what they were talking about once said that in learning to cast the first objective was to throw a straight line, and having once achieved this never, never to do it again. This is no more apposite than in Border fishing, where a straight line is asking for instantaneous drag. On most Border stretches there can be not just two but often several different current speeds between the rod and the fish, even if one is directly downstream of him (which is something to be avoided): to appear natural a dry fly must ride the current as though it is free and unattached; this can be achieved (but then often only for a short time) by its being on the end of a sufficiently wiggley line and leader to absorb the effects of the various current speeds; once the wiggles have been taken up and direct contact is established between the fly, and the line in a different current speed, the fly will be pulled along (or retarded) at a different speed from its own bit of current . . . drag.

There is, as usual, an exception to the no-drag rule, and this is when the angler is seeking to represent a sedge or similar insect scuttering across or against the current, and this is a case for imparting controlled drag to the fly in a manner emulating the natural insect; but this effect is unlikely to be produced by the accidental drag described above.

The best way I know of imparting a wiggley line is to start out as though trying to throw a straight one and at the last moment, as the line straightens, to lift the rod tip slightly; clearly one must have sufficient line out to carry it, if straight, some distance beyond the fish, otherwise the fly will finish up somewhere well short of him. Lest it be thought that there is a conflict between what I have just described and the follow-through described earlier, I must make it clear that the follow-through will follow immediately after the lifting of the rod tip which puts the wiggle in the line.

LINE SHOOTING

Shooting the line—the retention of a quantity of line in the left hand to be released just before the completion of the cast, so that it is carried out by the impetus of the remaining effort of the forward cast—is not really necessary in conventional casts over the distances we are envisaging. I do it, mainly from force of habit, but I do not subscribe to the belief that it necessarily makes for more delicate presentation—perhaps even to the contrary—and I am fairly certain that for a beginner it will probably give lower accuracy than straightforward off-the-reel casting.

However there are situations where the ability to shoot line can be advantageous; one of these is when it is necessary to increase range quickly from a nearby target to a fish some distance away, or when a longish cast has been made initially and a good downstream drift accomplished resulting in a quantity of line in hand; to repeat the exercise it saves a lot of false casting if all the loose line can be shot. If the room available for the back cast is substantially more restricted than the distance required for the forward—and it usually is—it is worthwhile to be able to false cast within the back cast length and finally shoot the extra line needed in front. But one of the most useful purposes to which line-shooting can be put is as an aid to producing a " shepherd's crook ".

THE SHEPHERD'S CROOK

I have indicated that it is not desirable to cast to a fish from directly downstream if it is at all avoidable: I think that this is something which goes without saying with most experienced anglers, but I do not recall having seen it set down with any degree of emphasis; we are often exhorted not to " line " a fish, but the best way of avoiding this—by casting to him from elsewhere than directly downstream—is usually omitted, perhaps as too elementary—except to a beginner.

A fish need not only be " lined " by the line but by the leader, and this much more frequently; to a fish a floating leader (or rather its indentation of the surface film) no matter how fine, looks like a streak of mercury, and the more directly overhead of him that it passes, the more alarming it must be. Let us now state un-equivocally that a fly, especially a dry fly, should if possible be presented to the fish upstream and to the side from which it is being cast: how far upstream must be judged on conditions and the speed of the current; the distance to the side will depend on how far an individual fish is prepared to move to acquire a par-ticular mouthful—the greater the better, from the angler's point of view since this avoids too close an initial inspection of the fly —but unfortunately the better the fish the less effort he is pre-pared to expend in seeking food, so that not much more than six inches should be aimed at.

Occasionally a situation is encountered when it is not possible to cast to a fish except from a position directly or nearly down-stream: to show him the fly upstream and even six inches to one side with a conventional cast must line him with the leader, and this is where our " shepherd's crook " cast comes in; it is equally useful for casts made less acutely to the current, for we are con-stantly told that the fish must see the fly before the leader, but not often told how.

If a right-handed side cast is executed with shooting line in hand, and the energy of the cast is such that more line than is available could be shot (in other words the line is brought up sharply against the reel or the hand which is holding it) two things should happen: firstly the line and leader having straightened in the air, they will fall back with the same wiggle which we ob-tained earlier by raising the rod tip; and second the fly, point, and some of the leader should come round in a left-handed semi-circle —the left-handed shepherd's crook. A similar effect can be achieved without shooting line if the line is tugged back gently as it straightens at the same time as the rod tip is lifted (not for-getting the follow-through), though I personally find this rather more difficult.

To accomplish a right-handed shepherd's crook it is necessary to have more line in hand than the energy of the cast can shoot, or to put it another way the cast should be made with insufficient power to take up all the shooting line, and this should result in the fly and point remaining curled back to the right: this is the right-handed shepherd's crook.

I would emphasise that the shepherd's crook just described refer to side casts carried out right-handed from the right; for the left-handed side cast, or back-handed cast executed on the left, opposites will apply. Shepherd's crook casts, especially accurate ones, are not perfected in five minutes; practice is required and also experimentation to get the right amount of force where it is required and also the right amount of slackness when that is needed.

CASTING A WIDE LOOP AND THE " FIGURE-OF-EIGHT "

The ever present Border problem of obstructed back cast can sometimes be overcome by throwing a wide loop at the rear. A conventional overheard cast has a comparatively narrow loop, though loop there must be unless the line is to be cracked like a whip and the fly never seen again; the loop is of course produced by ensuring that the tip of the rod describes an oval in its casting movement, the back cast being made in a plane a few degrees to the right of the ensuing forward cast; the movement of the rod from the back cast plane across to the forward cast plane allows the line to describe a loop before straightening, giving the fly also time to come round without harm; if this loop is too narrow or non-existent, either the line will drop as time is given to it to straighten or, if time is not given it to straighten the fly will be dragged round at such a speed that it will, literally, pass through the sound barrier, the sonic boom being the crack which signals the departure of the fly. However if a sufficiently wide loop is thrown to the rear by exaggerating the distance between the back- and forward-casting planes, it need not be necessary to allow the line to straighten at all but to come round in one continuous movement, and this is necessarily economical of back space; the exercise can be converted into a side cast simply by transferring the planes of movement sideways through about sixty degrees.

I must now admit that it is not strictly true to say that a side cast is " simply " an overhead cast executed sideways : in overhead casting the fly travels through an oval, but the fly in a side cast will often, without the angler realising it, describe a figure-of-eight. This results from the lifting of the rod to get the fly off the water, leaving the rod tip too high to follow the lower plane for the back cast and so remaining in the higher one; thus the forward cast automatically is made in the lower plane, and this is beneficial since it allows of gentler presentation.

This continuous figure-of-eight casting can be put to good use with a bit of practice: as described it is a vertical movement, with the figure-of-eight on edge; with a little application it can be converted into a horizontal movement with the " 8 " lying flat, and can be used to get a fly quite a long way under low-hanging obstacles in a manner not possible by other means.

THE ROLL CAST

The roll cast is well known and extremely useful when there is no room for a back cast at all; it is best begun with the rod inclined backward and outward over the right shoulder and the line hanging straight down from it to the water, but while the remainder of the line and the leader are still on the water upstream; if the rod is now punched forward the line will form itself into a hoop which will roll itself right along the line and leader, and if the rod is checked before the horizontal the whole lot should straighten in the air and the cast is completed as before.

One purpose for which the roll cast is ideally suited is the rapid and continuous presentation of an upstream wet fly or nymph, and it is well worthwhile perfecting one's technique for this reason alone. The sort of situation which calls for this method is when one is confronted with a stretch of rapid but apparently feature-less water in which it is difficult to pin-point a possible lie, and it is decided to search the water methodically. The procedure is naturally to comb the nearer water first, working in an arc and gradually lengthening line until it is safe to move a little upstream and begin again with a shorter line. The roll cast is made and the line allowed to come back at the speed of the current, while the rod tip is progressively raised to delay the moment when the belly is formed behind it which will accelerate the line; this can be helped by the simultaneous gathering of the line through the rings, though this is often not necessary except when a longer line is being cast: finally a point is reached when the belly has passed behind the caster and the loop is just right for a further roll cast, and this should be made without delay; the whole thing is a continuous process, and the most important factor, apart from ensuring that the line and fly are not allowed to drag, is undoubtedly timing. If line has been gathered during the retrieve this should be shot in the ensuing forward cast.

Because of the way in which it unrolls, it is difficult to complete a roll cast if the target is under low-hanging branches, and for this situation there is an alternative: sufficient of the line should be allowed to straighten out in the water downstream with the rod inclined backward at an angle of about 45° and held low; still low, the rod is punched forward through 90° to a point about 45° upstream and then followed through. In this cast there is still a tendency for the line to lift towards completion, and this can be guarded against by ensuring not only that the rod is kept low, but that its direction is inclined downward as it moves through its arc.

THE " BOUNCE-OFF "

A useful way of getting a fly to a fish with plenty of loose leader in a draggy situation is to bounce it off some convenient obstruction, if such exists: I am thinking particularly about the fish which is lying close against the outside of a bend in the far bank whose side is a sheer scour both above and below the surface. I can visualise many such places and the current pattern is more or less the same in each: at the angler's feet on the inside of the bend the water is slack and there may even be a back swim; further out the current becomes progressively faster and there is often an area of turbulence in midstream beyond which the water is moving very rapidly indeed until it reaches its fiercest a few inches from the far bank, and there there is a narrow strip of slightly slower current; and it is in that strip that we want our fly. It might do the trick if we put the fly in the adjacent very fast water, but it will probably be noticed that the naturals are eddying into the side, and it is there that most are being taken. If a convential cast is used, even with plenty of slack, and the fly is dropped into the relatively slow water right under the bank, it is likely to be whipped away at once by the fast water; if it is cast into the fast water itself it will almost immediately be retarded by the line or part of the leader still lying across slower water. If however, we draw off another yard of line and throw the fly against the vertical far bank there is a fair chance that much of the leader and certainly the point will finish within the slower strip (probably in a heap but with a bit of luck upstream of the fly) and thus allow the fly a few inches of untrammelled progress.

That is one example, but I have used the bounce-off method in any number of circumstances and against any number of different objects—rocks, tree stumps and roots, and once with great success all through a season against a stranded dredger bucket in the Usk, for a succession of trout who took up position partially inside it.

DOWNSTREAM WET FLY

With regard to across-and-down wet fly casting, I have little original to add to what is probably already known: it is a method which I employ for trout in early spring when I am on a bigger river, when I use two or sometimes three flies, or more frequently during the winter proper for grayling on smaller waters where one fly is quite enough to handle. As I have already mentioned I use a sinking line for this purpose, and the cast should be made so as firstly to assist the line to sink rapidly, and subsequently to present the flies to the fish in as natural a manner as is possible. Both of these purposes are again best served by the casting of a loose line: a straight line which is gripped at once by the current will never have a chance to sink and the flies will immediately be slashed across the current until they come to rest straight downstream.

Each situation calls for a differing approach, but as a general rule the best casting angle is about 45° downstream: it is often necessary to cast squarer than this to persuade the line to sink more deeply, and if this is done, in addition to mending the line as soon as it touches the water an attempt should be made to cast an upstream bow in the line; this is done by giving the rod tip an upstream twitch just before the line settles on the water, so that what is needed is really two successive upstream flicks, one in the air and one on the surface. Remember that unlike a floating line, a sinker cannot be mended once it is underwater, so that to achieve a similar effect—the slowing down of the flies as they swing across the current—it is wise to have two or three yards of loose line in hand, to be released progressively as the flies are felt to accelerate.

Fish will often follow the fly across the current and the most popular taking point is usually at an acute downstream angle: other fish will often lie and look at the fly as it hangs in the water at the end of the swim, and grab it at the beginning of the re-trieve when they think it is about to escape; it is wise therefore always to begin the retrieve gently, and even to agitate the fly a little by moving the rod tip before actually starting to retrieve.

AMBIDEXTEROUS CASTING

As I mentioned earlier when describing the shepherd's crook casts, I did so from the point of view of the right handed man, as in-deed I have done with all other aspects of tackle handling: this seems reasonable since the majority of us *are* right-handed and I have no doubt that left-handed people reading such descriptions automatically make the appropriate adjustments to suit their own way of doing things. Nevertheless an ambidexterous angler is in a position of great advantage and much envied by those who are confined to single-handed use of their tackle; nowadays when one's fishing rights are so often confined by tenure to single banks of rivers, or on Border streams where as often as not only one bank or the other is fishable, and that usually alternating, the single-handed angler is likely to be at a disadvantage for an average of 50% of his fishing. Back-handed casting is perhaps the easier expedient, but not in my view the best, since it is incapable of getting out of the tackle the performance for which it was de-signed, with delicacy and accuracy suffering in consequence. Far better to resolve to make oneself ambidexterous, and this is not so difficult for most of us as it sounds; the greatest obstacle is convincing oneself that it can be done at all!

I am sure that the best way to begin is to have a similar rod and line in each hand; start casting with the right and let the left move in unison with it, paralleling its motions. This is a popular parlour trick, but it is surprising how easy it is (although it always looks very clever) because opposite limbs will always try and move in co-ordination with each other rather than in discon-cert; it is a simple thing to move both arms in a circle in the same direction but needs concentration to do so in opposite directions, or to move one in a circle and the other up and down.

Having perfected your two-handing casting—or at any rate got it going reasonably well—put down the right-hand rod and con-tinue with the left; at first it will go hay-wire and perserverance is needed, with every now and then recourse to both rods to bring you back on the rails. This, like so many other worthwhile things, requires patience and practice, but once accomplished will pay dividends far greater than the trouble taken in mastering it.

LINE CONTROL

Before leaving casting, reference must be made to the handling of the line once the cast has been completed: while emphasising the need for a loosely laid line in upstream Border fishing, I must also emphasise the need for close control over it at all times; indeed the looser the cast the closer the subsequent control must be, for with a take anticipated at any time there is a lot of slack line to be got off the water in tightening on the fish. The angler must begin to gather in line in his left hand the moment the fly touches the water; if he delays he may quickly find that he has lost control and cannot get his slack in fast enough, in which case his best recourse is to strip the line in through the rings and drop it in the water until he is again in touch. At best the lack of instantaneous control can result in a missed fish, but at worst he can put down every fish in a pool, for if a belly is allowed to form in the line below the rod tip and the current gets hold of that belly, the fly can be ripped across the pool like a speedboat.

Line can be gathered either by figure-of-eighting in the palm of the left hand or by coiling: I personally use the former because it allows the line to be fed back in a trouble-free and controlled manner when recasting, though it may not be so good for the line; coiling can result in an embarrassing if not complicated tangle particularly during the subsequent cast. Simply dropping retrieved line in the water is not to be recommended if only because it often manages to get itself tangled round something, usually when one has a fish on. Of course in very fast water there is frequently no time to do anything but strip the line in and drop it in the water, but if the latter is done circumspectly the very speed of the current should keep the retrieved line out of trouble.

While the foregoing has been written primarily with the dry fly in mind, it applies for the most part also to the upstream wet fly or nymph: a measure of drag is sometimes acceptable with this method, and on occasion this can be turned to advantage by the use of a nymph in places where surface drag conditions preclude a dry fly altogether—I have in mind the tail of a pool, where a quickening current right across the stream will start a dry fly accelerating the moment it touches the water, unless it can be fished square across, which would be unusual. Nevertheless it is wise in general to try and avoid drag in a wet fly or nymph as sedulously as in a dry fly; there is no justification for a more careless presentation of a nymph, especially since its moment to moment movements cannot be observed like those of a dry fly. Time must be given to a nymph to enable it to sink to the depth at which it is required to fish, and to accomplish this perhaps a looser line than for a dry fly may be required, and this will call for an even prompter assumption of control on completion of the cast.

When a fish is hooked, manifestly there must be no more slack line: in order to maintain tight control the line should be drawn in with the left hand and prevented from going out again by being trapped between the fingers of the right and the butt of the rod. It is unusual but not exactly rare to have to give line to a Border fish (although I know of some grayling which justify it), and it is also unwise to do so except *in extremis,* since snags are never far away. The occasion for playing a Border fish off the reel is not common, if only because there is usually loose line in hand at the time of the take and the risks involved in holding the fish while the spare line is got back on the reel are not often justified: when a really good fish does connect, however, those risks may have to be taken, and the fingers of the right hand will be working overtime in holding the rod, controlling the fish and also maintaining some sort of tension on the loose line to ensure that it gets back on the reel in some sort of order; this is assuming that the reel is left-hand wind—if it is right-handed than all this complicated work must be done with the left hand! It is hardly necessary to point out, of course, that a good fisherman should not be caught out in this way, since his watercraft should tell him that such a fish is in the offing even if he cannot see it, and he would make the appropriate anticipatory dispositions; nevertheless it can and does happen to the best of us.

TIGHTENING

" Striking " is a word that I do not like in the context of Border fishing: by definition it implies a violent and sweeping movement which, while applicable in other types of angling such as sea fishing or long-range freshwater fishing is nevertheless wholly out of place in the activity we are here discussing. Personally I prefer " tightening " and that is the term which I propose to employ hereafter. Tightening on a Border fish must of course be firm, but having regard to the fineness of the point and the often restricted field of movement for the rod, must also be controlled. I find it a good plan to try not to involve the wrist when I tighten, but to move the forearm and rod as one; if the wrist is allowed to pivot the effect on the rod tip can be considerably exaggerated. Even within the limits imposed by controlled tightening it is possible for a nervous or over-eager angler to inject a great deal of force into the action—I make no claim for exception—and where this propensity is recognised it is a wise precaution to be prepared to tighten " off the reel " if there is no spare line in hand; or if there is, which is more common, to be gripping the line sufficiently loosely to allow enough to be drawn through to cushion the shock.

On the problem of timing in tightening there is little advice that I am able or prepared to offer, since circumstances differ so widely between waters, fish and individuals. When fishing a wet fly or nymph the response should usually be immediate, or sooner, to any indication of the possible attention of a fish: this may show as a distinct drawing forward of the leader, but more often can be recognised only as a brief stopping or similar faint unnatural movement, akin to dragging in reverse, leaving one to speculate (if one was not quick enough) " was that a fish or wasn't it?" More rarely in Border fishing is the movement of the fish seen, either as a brief flash (more common in grayling, this) or as a faintly discernible displacement of surface water in the case of a near-surface feeder.

Experienced nymph fishermen will be seen to tighten as if by reflex, usually successfully, in response to no apparent stimulus: when questioned they may confess to not knowing why they tightened, or say that they sensed a fish. There is no magical explanation to this, for such men *know* that a fish is there, and their intuitive knowledge is simply a heightened awareness of the signs, derived from watercraft and years of watching for fish to take flies.

Tightening with a dry fly is in some respects less of a problem, because usually it can be seen to be taken: even this, though, is not invariable in streamy water: on a light-dappled surface the fly can simply disappear and one is left wondering if it was sucked under by a fish or by the current or if it is still there but obscured by the interplay between the ripples and the light. However, assuming that the rise to the dry fly has been seen (it should have been anticipated anyway) the timing of the angler's response is very much something which the angler must determine for himself in the light of his own experience on his own waters. The axiom is: the larger the fish and the slower the water the greater the pause before tightening: on Border water the pause will rarely be very great and often there will be no perceptible pause at all. This is really something which works itself out in its own time: an angler who concludes that he is missing more fish than he should will try to tighten more quickly or more slowly, depending on his own judgment of what he may be doing wrong.

I would mention here an eventuality which I find fairly common, especially in less turbulent places: it is when fish splash at and drown a dry fly, sometimes coming out of the water and down on it like a rainbow trout will, but without connecting. For a long time this practice perplexed me until an idea emerged from the recesses of my mind—probably something I had read in the past though it could have been original thought—and I resolved that the next time it happened I would refrain from tightening for a full two seconds of time after the splash: this in fact I did— with the exercise of monumental self control—and my fish was on! By hindsight, of course, the answer is clear: for some reason the fish did not want to eat a floating fly and decided to transform it into a sunk one before coming back for it, but any explanation for this behaviour could never pass beyond conjecture.

THE UPSTREAM NYMPH

Mechanically speaking the methods of fishing dry flies and downstream wet flies are fairly universal: what you do on one stream you will do on most others, with minor concessions to the speed and variability of the flow. There can be, however, differences in the handling of the upstream nymph in the context of Border stream fishing, which are also to be found in the use of the North Country upstream wet fly: indeed wet flies used for upstream

Border fishing *are* mainly North Country spider patterns, and are worked in substantially the same way as nymphs.

Very many Border anglers are exclusively dry fly men—I was myself for a long time—and there is no doubt in my own mind that the dry fly is far and away the most satisfying of all methods of catching fish; to watch one's fly (especially if it is one's own creation) drifting down on the current until a fish rises to intercept it provides a visual pleasure which to me has few equals, and one which I never tire of experiencing: it has its parallel in the coarse fisherman who prefers to sit and " read " the expressive tip of his float, even when circumstances tell him that he might get more and better fish by legering, and simply watch his rod-tip or feel his line.

Nevertheless the fact has to be faced that less—sometimes much less—than half the fish-holding surface area of a Border stream is fishable with a dry fly; back currents, turbulence, the pull-off at the tails of pools—all of which can be classified under a single expressive heading—" drag "—deny whole areas of productive water to the dry-fly-only man: paradoxically such places often hold the best fish, and not by accident either, for on a hard fished water where the method is predominantly dry fly certain fortunate fish wax large and unmolested simply because they cannot be effectively covered. Not only current conditions restrict the use of the dry fly; its lightness, abetted by the air resistance of its dressing, both of which are essential to the delicacy with which it must be delivered, all contribute to a gentle descent onto the water during which the most accurately cast fly is subject to the influence of the lightest airs: because of this many productive spots are denied to the dry fly because of the narrowness of the entry—among the emergent twigs of a submerged tree, between a hanging branch and the bank, and in the narrow channels through a weed-bed— let the breeze increase to more than a zephyr and such places tend to multiply!

A nymph, and especially a weighted nymph, suffers from few such disabilities; virtually the whole of the fishable area of a stream is available to it: while there are some places in which it may be difficult to persuade it to work in a life-like manner there are very few in which its use—or perhaps misuse—will actually frighten fish, though the same cannot be said of a dry fly when the line is caught in a violent drag-current. Just as a natural nymph can move in a manner differing from that of an inanimate object in accord with the current—faster or slower than the flow, across it or even against it (the free-swimming, surface-hatching nymphs of the various olive duns and the iron blue all dart about as agilely as tiny fish)—so an artificial nymph or wet fly can perform the same manoeuvres and in the process attract fish. Where the stream comes brawling through a narrow neck into a deep pool there is usually a back eddy on one or both sides of the turbulent water just inside the head (and usually the deepest part) of the pool; only a beginner would attempt to put a dry fly onto one of the back eddies, although the experienced angler would know that the best fish in the pool is likely to be nearby, and would be unlucky not to get an answer to his nymph in such a place.

Clearly the placing of the nymph by the cast must be such as to give it the best opportunity of behaving naturally in accordance with the conditions obtaining in a particular place, and involuntary drag, a degree of which I have already said to be acceptable, must be kept to a minimum; there is no more room for the careless handling of a nymph than of a dry fly. In places of narrow entry so hazardous to a dry fly a nymph can be placed with an accuracy commensurate with the skill of the caster; its weight and lack of air-resistance make it impervious to reasonable wind conditions because its likely deflection can be estimated and adjusted. To sum up, there is almost nowhere—given the ability to put a fly on the water at all—on an average Border stream that is not fishable with a nymph, and it is often capable of being cut into places where a dry fly has not a hope.

An upstream nymph also offers a much better chance of success in extremes of water conditions—perhaps surprisingly when the water is thin and clear, and more predictably when there is a cocoa-coloured flood. When a long drought has reduced the stream to a gin-clear trickle, a small nymph, fished delicately and as fine and as far-off as possible, can fetch fish from under roots and the deeper runnels where the daintiest dry fly will send them panicking. When heavy and continuous rain has turned the river into a turbid, turgid flood, and dry flies even if they can be seen are ignored, a large dark nymph or wet fly (a Black-and-Peacock Spider is useful) will often produce as good results as when the flow is normal; under these conditions too of course, a down-and-across wet fly should also bring success. The nymph fisherman, then, is an all-water and an all-weather fisherman, but is also deprived of the excuses which normally come as a corollary to unfavourable conditions!

The conventional way (that is the chalk stream way) of fishing a nymph is to do so in much the same manner as with a dry fly, that is to cast it above and to the near side of one's fish on a leader greased to permit it to fish at the required depth, and to tighten when the fish having accepted the fly is seen to turn away again, or when the leader is seen to draw. That great nymph fisherman, the late Major Oliver Kite, publicised the " induced take " for the benefit of fish which ignored the passing nymph; as the nymph approaches the fish the rod top is raised to cause the fly slightly to change course—to give it the impression of being alive and seeking to escape. Although this " dry fly" method of fishing the nymph can be quite successful on Border waters, especially in rougher stretches, it suffers from a fundamental disability: on a chalk stream or other more placid rivers even if both the fish and the nymph cannot actually be seen, their respective positions can be judged with tolerable accuracy. While watercraft and acute observation will often tell the Border angler roughly where a fish ought to be, it would be an extremely clever man who could claim to know exactly where his *nymph* was at any given moment in order accurately to time his induced take. The answer, once arrived at, makes the problem seem simple in retrospect: it is to fish the nymph as a continuous series of induced takes, or, put another way, to fish an " agitated nymph ": where an inert nymph or wet fly, drifting like a submerged dry fly, may pass a fish and leave it uninterested, such a fish can rarely resist one which has movement and the apparent means of eluding him—hence the success of the induced take—; since on Border water the precise whereabouts both of the fish and the nymph are usually matters of uncertainty, a continuous inducement of the nymph must ensure that it is in movement whenever it happens to come within the orbit of a fish.

I have found that the best way of imparting agitation to my nymph is to keep my rod top in continuous movement through an arc of not more than six inches, at the same time gathering loose line in my left hand in order to keep in close touch with the fly; the rod itself is held fairly low and at an angle to the line—this to cushion the effect of a potential (though unfortunately very rare) smash take by a heavy fish. It is not a good practice to impart movement and at the same time shorten line by a progressive raising of the rod tip in short jerks, because should the take come when the rod is approaching the vertical there is often not sufficient leeway left to ensure firm tightening and subsequent control. The degree of movement to be imparted to a nymph will be governed by the speed and turbulence of the water: in rough water it may need to be very little, provided that the left hand is kept in fairly close touch with the fly, because the water will do much of the work for you; but in a slow and placid pool it is often necessary to induce considerable agitation. The continuous movement of the nymph, and the close control which must involuntarily accompany it, does much to iron out any problems of tightening: after all one is actually tightening with every short up-stroke of the rod; this is particularly valuable with the hit-and-spit tactics of the grayling, though not so critical with trout, who can hang on to an untightened nymph for a surprisingly long time (especially, oddly enough, larger fish)—much longer than they will hold a dry fly.

Chapter Five

WATERCRAFT

WATERCRAFT MIGHT be defined simply as a faculty for knowing where a fish is likely to be combined with the ability to catch him: what a world of meaning can be encompassed by one small sentence! Watercraft is a collective noun for the amalgam of a diversity of instincts and acquired skills: no one is born with it, some achieve it so easily that often they don't realise, in so many words, that they have it (such men are often known as " otters "), most of us have to serve a long apprenticeship to attain a measure of it, and a few never have it and wouldn't know what it is anyway. Without watercraft one cannot begin to be a whole fisherman and yet to have it one has first of all to be a whole fisherman —not in the sense of being an expert caster and fly dresser, which are manual skills—but in respect for and understanding of one's opponent. A successful general makes his " appreciation of the situation " primarily by putting himself in his adversary's position and saying: " on the information available to me what would I do in his place?" He strives to think like his antagonist and never makes the mistake of underrating him. The military tactician is fortunate in that his opponent is a member of the same species; it is much simpler for a man to think like another man and not nearly so easy for him to think like a fish, and yet this is really what watercraft is about.

In talking about thinking like a fish—or any other animal— let me make it quite clear that I do not mean in the anthropomorphic way to which so many of the human race are prone. An extraordinary number of people invest animals with similar if reduced (a big concession this!) powers of thought and reasoning, and mental and physical sensation, to their own: this is typified by the often heard expression: " how would *you* like someone to do that to you?" To think like a fish means to try and think like a fish *thinks* (and " think " is here very loosely applied; perhaps a better word would be " react ") and not to think as a man would were he a fish.

One factor in our favour is that in considering how a fish " thinks " we do not mean that it has the capacity for reasoning; it reacts instinctively to stimuli, either from within itself (hunger, need for oxygen) or from outside (fear of predators, own predatory instinct): also a fish can learn, and an old cannibal on hard fished water must have learned a lot.

But before we can understand how a fish is reacting at any given time we must first of all know much more about him: how he sees, hears and smells; what makes him comfortable and uncomfortable; what he fears (apart from the obvious) and what degrees of fear he experiences from various sources of fear, and how long it takes to forget about it; what he likes to eat at any given time and how much effort he is prepared to make to get it.

The comprehensive answers merely to these few questions would tax the qualifications of a far more ambitious work than this; I shall sketch some answers in lightly as far as my own capability permits, but my main purpose in posing the questions in the first place is rather to set the reader enquiring for himself, so that what answers emerge are not merely academic ones but are based on the reader's own research, and thus doubly valid in their contribution to his watercraft.

How does one go about finding how a fish sees and hears? Some enthusiasts equip themselves with breathing apparatus and actually go down and join the fish, and while this expedient has much to recommend it it is perhaps best left to the really dedicated. However one can make a start simply by submerging oneself in one's own bathwater (while it is still clean, of course), and while looking upward one can float things across one's vision, and note that a man can have a window just like a fish : while thus submerged one can bang the side of the bath both above and below the surface and note the difference in the sounds. Useful experience can be gained in a swimming bath, or even by looking up at the surface of a tropical fish tank with one's eyes close to the glass side while drawing a dry fly across the surface film.

SIGHT

We can accept with a fair degree of certainty that a trout under water (though I am less certain about grayling) can see the same things in substantially the same way as a man can see under water, and that in normal light he can see the same colours, though possibly more colours as well, since there is evidence that a trout's spectral range may be greater than ours: we know that he can see much better than we can at night, although not in colour.

A fish's eyes function independently of each other, and much of its general viewing is done monocularly which gives it a very wide field of vision with one eye or the other: the area in which the visions of both eyes overlap is comparatively narrow—about 36° in front, rather less overhead and tapering off towards the rear—and while for ordinary purposes it can see all that it needs to all round itself (except for the " blind " areas behind and below it), to take a fly it needs to turn into its binocular field in order accurately to judge its distance.

I have a strong suspicion that the monocular vision of a grayling is less acute than that of a trout, and if this is so then one or two enigmas connected with the former would fall into place: I have often become aware of the presence of a grayling happily feeding in shallow water right alongside me, and close enough to be poked with my rod, and have caught him there—something which I cannot visualise happening with a sane trout (or could it be that a trout in a similar situation is also not able to see the angler, but would be activated by the stimulus of another sense, such as hearing, which a grayling might ignore?).

There is also the very narrow but comparatively long taking area of the grayling: a trout is usually prepared to move as far to the side as he is forward or to the rear in order to take a fly—more if he is hungry—but a grayling cannot be persuaded out of his narrow strip although the longitudinal area through which he is prepared to move to a fly is much greater than that of a trout. In this latter observation I have the confirmation of no less a grayling fanatic than Charles Ritz, in his book " A Flyfisher's Life "[1]; he probably knows more about grayling than I shall ever learn, and while I cannot go along with quite all his conclusions in the

[1] " A Flyfisher's Life ". Charles Ritz; Max Reinhardt, London.

context of my own Border fishing, it has to be remembered that our respective waters, not to put too fine a point on it, differ considerably.

If a grayling's lateral vision is inferior, can the converse be true and its binocular vision be more acute? Certainly it is more difficult to approach grayling from behind and they are more easily scared by lining or a clumsily presented fly. Eugene V. Connett[1] points out that a trout's eye is not completely round but that the pupil extends slightly towards the front, and suggests that this may be of assistance in its binocular vision; but a grayling's eye greatly exaggerates this characteristic and is positively pear-shaped (although most illustrators show it as quite round): if Connett's hypothesis is valid it is likely to be even more germane to the grayling than to the trout. It must be remembered that when either fish is looking forward, and to a lesser extent upward, it is looking out of the corners of its eyes, even allowing for its ability to swivel its eyeballs; it is likely therefore that a trout sees more clearly sideways, out of one eye, than forward out of two. This could account for the fact that a trout, differing from a grayling, comes better to a fly, natural or artificial, which passes slightly to one side of him rather than bang overhead: nevertheless he will always turn and come to it full face, indicating that he requires his binocular vision primarily for precise judgement of distance but also for closer inspection. This suggests that a trout may be somewhat shortsighted when looking to the front and depend on its monocular vision for long sight while the grayling, possibly because of the conformation of its eye, tends to the opposite.

THE WINDOW AND THE MIRROR

The fish's window is an optical fact; it is something which is apparent to any eye looking upward from beneath the water and is governed by the laws of reflection and refraction of light: it is the area of surface through which a fish can see the world above the surface, as opposed to the very much larger area of surface that it cannot see through and which appears to it as a mirror. Since the fish is aware of the approach of surface food whether it is on the mirror or the window, the latter is really more important

[1] " My Friend the Trout ". Eugene V. Connett 3rd. D. Van Nostrand Co. Inc. New Jersey.

to the fisherman than to the fish, because it is through the window that the fish can see him.

The window may be imagined as the base of a shallow inverted cone, the apex of which is the fish's eye: the angle of the apex is constant at rather more than 90°: thus the deeper the fish lies the bigger his window and the shallower the smaller it becomes, but this variation in size has no effect on the amount that he can see through it, since the overall "picture" is either magnified or diminished; clearly when a fish is lying near the surface the images seen through his window must be tiny, which is probably why he is more easily approachable.

The existence of the window is itself of less importance than the reason for it—the refraction of light; when light passes into water—or out of it—unless it does so at an exact right-angle it is bent, and the greater the divergence from the right-angle the greater the bend. If you thrust the end of your rod into the water it appears to be broken; the part under water seems to be bent up towards the surface and foreshortened: for the same reason an observed fish is always deeper, nearer and probably bigger than it looks. (It is wise never to forget this, and occasionally to remind oneself of it by sticking one's rod end in the water; for if you cast to a visible fish where it appears to be you are almost sure to line him over where he really is.)

Apart from the submerged rod top, one of the most impressive ways I know of demonstrating the effect of refracted light in water is with the aid of the bathroom wash-basin. The observer should place himself, probably kneeling, so that the plug is just hidden from his eyes by the lip of the basin: he should then turn on the tap, and as the basin fills with water the plug will be seen to rise into view; as the basin is emptied the plug-hole will sink out of sight again. One conclusion to be drawn from this is that a fish and a fisherman can be looking at each other although there may be a solid object in a direct line between them.

Refraction works in reverse from the fish's point of view, but its effect is very much more exaggerated; he sees the angler and his rod as much shorter but no thinner and somewhere up in the air. Although a fat airborne dwarf is alarming enough, perhaps more significant is the rod tip which if held vertical will seem to the fish to be directly overhead, shorter but no thinner; compare it with a rod held low and horizontal—if seen at all the concentration of refracted rays will have flattened it almost into invisibility—and draw an obvious conclusion.

It is possible, though not easy, to keep underneath the view from the window, since light striking the water at an acute angle is reflected off it and not refracted to the fish. In reverse this is the explanation of the fish's window, for he cannot see through the surface at an angle of less than just over 40° to it; since this obtains in all directions around him he has a circular window. However to keep out of the window a man would need to be standing level with the water at least twenty yards away, and fifteen yards even if kneeling. This presupposes flat calm water; add only a small ripple and we are back to the drawing board for both the fisherman and the fish, since the areas of vision though broken up (which the fish is used to) are then greatly extended.

The window in no way assists the fish in alerting him to the approach of surface food, since he will be aware of it while it is still outside its compass; it *is* likely to enable him at the last moment to decide whether to accept or reject upon close inspection. We have already learned that the fish sees the underside of the surface beyond the window as a mirror; an insect resting on the surface will produce a light pattern on the underside of it where its feet and any other part of it in contact with the surface make an impression on the surface film, and this is seen as a cluster of brilliant sparks of light: no part of a normally resting insect will penetrate the film, so that nothing will be seen apart from its light pattern.

In the case of a drowned insect or a hatching fly, of course the film will be penetrated, so that in addition to a degree of light pattern the fish will see that portion of the insect which is below the surface, although this is likely also to have a silvery sheen, since the water-repellant properties of most insects, especially hatching ones, invest them with a fine integument of air: apart from this the subsurface portion of the insect, unless it is very translucent, will appear as a dark outline against the bright mirror, and little actual colour will be apparent.

It will be seen from this that it is important to make a distinction in the way in which one is fishing one's fly in regard to what one is trying to imitate: a well oiled dry fly of steely hackles cocked delicately on its tip-toes is unlikely to be of avail when fish are concerning themselves with insects which are on the point either of hatching or foundering, and experience has taught me that it is the latter types which are of far the greatest importance in Border fishing.

The fish then has noted the imminence of a potential mouthful; if it is going to drift into his window he has little to do but wait for it, but (in the case of a trout) if it is going to pass outside of the window he will have to take the window to it, and place the fly and the centre of the window on, so to speak, a collision course. A grayling will rarely rise obliquely to a fly passing on the flank of his window, though he might drift laterally across the bottom until his window is centred on the insect so that it will pass directly over him, and rise to it from there.

It is interesting to close one's eyes and try to imagine how a fish sees a fly coming out of the mirror into its window; there is of course no *sudden* change because the two areas blend over a wide band, especially in agitated surface conditions, so that really there are three stages—full mirror, transitional and full window —and in a ripple there will be strips of mirror moving continuously right across the window: in the case of an up-winged dun the first thing to appear above the surface in the window will be the tip of the wings like the mast-head of a yacht, and remembering the refraction it will be seen as high in the air and much more frontally than in a straight line from fish to fly. Had I not already satisfied myself otherwise I would say that this was a cogent argument for the winging of dry flies imitating these species, or at least for a single, central upright and forward wing, but certainly on my own waters I do not believe that it makes any difference at all.

After the wing tip the rest of the fly will progressively come into view, working downward, and at the same time the exaggerated height of the wings will be decreased until the composite insect will appear flatter than normal; meanwhile the frontal view will become modified downward as the fly approaches the centre of the window at which point the fish will have the most " normal " view of it since being directly overhead it will be subject to least optical aberration (though if a trout he should have taken it by now!).

Once a surface fly is in the window it must not be assumed that the light pattern of the mirror ceases—it does not—it is simply modified to take its place among the additional factors obtaining, such as colour, but the overriding impression is still of sparkle. Since the tips of the insect's legs are still in their light pattern-forming depressions, all that can be seen of them throughout are points of white light; it is thus arguable whether the hackle colour, and notably the hackle-tip colour, of a truly dry fly is of great significance as far as imitating legs is concerned.

A surface insect which is observed by a fish in its window is seen in transmitted light; that is to say the light passes through the fly (if it can) in order to reach the fish; it is, as we say, seen against the light: body translucence and transmitted colour therefore, if they exist, are important, and these factors must be given careful attention in an artificial if they obtain in the natural which is to be imitated; size and outline are important, but the most perfect exact-imitation (seen in reflected light) is likely to fail if it is hard-outlined and opaque when seen against the light, and this is possibly why the tried and tested Border patterns, " general " though they may be, but *impressionistic*, are so markedly successful.

Much that I have written above concerning the window is slanted from the trout's point of view rather than the grayling's : what both see in their respective mirrors and windows must be substantially the same (with reservations regarding the grayling's side-sight) but usually from different positions and initiating differing reactions. Grayling prefer to lie close to the bottom, and will often still be there when trout have moved to mid water or are even poised for sustained surface feeding; it is quite rare ever to find a Border grayling in the latter position. Although he must see the fly long before a trout lying above him, a grayling will wait until it is right overhead—in other words in the centre of his large window—before starting to rise to it; then as every grayling fisher knows, he will come up at it with a rush and if he doesn't miss it altogether will take it at a point downstream of his lie, to which he will return immediately as fast as he came up.

The low-lying grayling with his relatively large window can give rise to a number of thoughts : one is that the big window provides bigger images of objects, such as anglers, in the outside world; another is that he has a much longer scrutiny of the fly, both outside his window and in it (and also of the leader if the fly is counterfeit) especially since he delays his rise until top-dead-centre; in spite of this his view of the fly is a much more distant one (better forward binocular vision at long range?) even though in general grayling prefer smaller artificials than trout; his attack on the fly—I cannot think of a more descriptive word—is such that he is left no time for close examination, both of which suggest that his near sight upward is not his strong point.

UNDER THE MIRROR

A fish's view of a nymph or other sub-aquatic animal is governed by quite different factors from those concerned with surface food, and is in many respects much more complex; much will depend on whether he is seeing it above or below him or on the same level; on the colour of the river bed and whether it is less or more reflective than the surface mirror: for most of a fish's sightings of under surface creatures will be in the area beneath the mirror, and only rarely will a trout still be interested in it if it has got as far as entering the sub-aquatic area of the window cone and be affected, like a surface insect, primarily by transmitted light (though a grayling will often take a nymph in that area).

Creatures under water in a fish's mirror field will always be seen twice—once in the flesh, so to speak, and also upside down in the mirror—this applies also to everything else in the stream— the stones and weeds of the river bed and not least the angler's waders; no doubt many an unsuspecting caddis-grub crawling on the bottom has met its end as a result of having first been detected in the surface mirror. One wonders if a fish is born with the instinct for knowing which of the two images he sees is the real one and which is the reflection, or if he has to learn it the hard way as a fingerling.

Fish see underwater animals mainly in reflected light (that is light shining on them rather than through them) and the main source of this is from above them through the surface, but it can also be from below as a result of surface light being reflected back off the bottom: this returning bottom light will bring with it the colour of the bottom, which as well as affecting the apparent colour of a nymph will itself be reflected in the mirror, and so on.

If a length of stream bed is an unusual colour, say yellow, because it is reflecting yellow light but absorbing all other colours, there is no suggestion that there should be special nymph patterns for that particular stretch, since the naturals also will be affected by the same underwater yellow light: however the example high-lights the fact that artificials must be so constructed as to reflect light in the same way as the naturals, and this is mainly a matter of texture; two artificial flies made of different materials from the same dye bath will reflect another colour in different ways if the textures of the materials are different—for example quill and wool—and in extreme cases may actually appear as different colours. I have quoted quill and wool because both are used widely in successful nymph patterns, often together in the same pattern, and this can only mean that both are good texturally for reflecting all lights in the same way as those parts of the naturals which each is used to copy—generally the quill for the abdomen and wool for the thorax—but we will go into this in more detail in the chapter on artificial flies.

Transmitted light is also a factor in the fish's view of a nymph, especially if the creature is above the level of the fish, for it will then be seen against the bright background of the mirror and any translucency of its body will be apparent.

Unlike a surface insect which (unless it is scuttering across the water in order to try and get off it) moves in unison with the patch of surface on which it is sitting, a nymph can move independently of the current—though not by a great deal if it is a swift one—; it may attempt to swim against it or fight its way across it and also (and this more rarely except in slower reaches) can go with it, adding its own small momentum to that of the stream and actually travelling a little faster than the current: it can also move through the third dimension denied to the surface fly—up and down. This is of course why a measure of drag may be tolerated in a wet fly or nymph but not in a dry fly.

SUNLIGHT

Before leaving consideration of a fish's sight there is one other very important factor to be explored, namely the effect of direct sunlight on a fish and an angler's deployment of himself and his tackle in relation to that effect.

Time and again I have seen it stated flatly that the best approach to a fish in sunny conditions (to avoid throwing a shadow) is from the side away from the sun—that is to say to place the fish between one's self and the sun—and I cannot think of a more dangerous piece of advice.

For the purpose of my argument I am presupposing that the position of the sun is generally to one side or the other of the fish: were it directly in front of him he would have difficulty in seeing to feed at all and would be very uncomfortable; if it is directly behind him it is neutral anyway and ideally placed from the fish's point of view. We have established already that fish's vision to the side is monocular and that its eyes function independently of each other; now we must add that the pupils of a fish's eyes cannot contract as ours do in order to exclude brighter light, nor does its eye have lids which it can narrow or close for the same purpose. It follows then that when direct sunlight falls onto a fish's eye there is nothing he can do but accept temporary blindness in that eye, and this is one very good reason why fish prefer to lie in the shade. With one eye out of action in this way the other becomes doubly effective on its own side; not only does it have the fish's undivided attention but everything that it sees is bathed in the full reflected light of the sun; and this is the side from which it is suggested that we approach the fish! To the angler on the sunny side of the fish sombre clothing and a dark background will be of little avail, for the difference in texture between his clothes and his background will still cause him to be obtrusive. The conclusion to be drawn therefore is that in sunny conditions, especially if it is bright sun, the best position for an angler is on the side of the fish blinded by the sun, always provided that his shadow does not fall on the fish or in any area within the visual range of the unaffected eye—and allowance must here be made for the fish's possible movement from side to side in the water.

The fly must naturally be presented on the sighted side if it is to be seen at all, and to do this we must depart from a principle which I have earlier been at pains to establish, namely that one should present a fly on the same side of the fish as that from which one is casting in order to avoid the risk of lining him with the leader. In this circumstance the fly must be presented on the farther side of the fish from the angler, and I have to say frankly that I know of no ready-made formula for doing it easily beyond what I have already written: remember that we *may* not be able to see the fish at all; much more likely in Border fishing his location has been indicated either by a rise-form or by a calculation based on watercraft. An accurate shepherd's crook cast is called for, delivered from as square a position as is practicable, and the fly placed so as to drift as close as possible to the offside of the fish. in order to minimise the amount of traversing leader which will drift across the effective vision of the fish should the fly not be taken first time. Personally I usually give first consideration to a nymph in this circumstance, since the sunken leader is likely to be slightly less obtrusive than a floating one.

I must emphasise that I have discussed this problem in the connotation of *bright* sunlight, and the conclusions must be progressively modified as the brightness is diminished, for we must bear in mind the slight possibility (in the absence of evidence to the contrary) that evolution over aeons of time may have left fish better equipped for staring into the sun than ourselves. Nevertheless my own empiric experience has shown me that the basis of the argument is valid in all conditions of bright light where the light on one side of a fish, even when not originating from direct sunshine, is brighter than on the other. In this context I must exclude a situation where one side of a river is quite open and the other packed with trees whose overhead branches spread across the water; the open bank, even if it is to the North and the sun is shining on the other side of the trees, will be not only the direction from which the strong light originates but effectively the *only* source of light. The main danger here will be that the angler may loom as a dark silhouette against a contracted field of light—much as he would were he entering the mouth of a cave—and appear more obvious (and more ominous) to the fish than if he were wearing cricketing flannels in bright sunshine.

HEARING

When we come to think about what a fish hears we are not considering hearing in the sense that we know it—through our ears. A fish has ears, it is true, but their use is confined mainly to the secondary purpose which all ears (including our own) serve, namely the maintenance of equilibrium—a sort of built-in spirit level—without which we would fall down and a fish would keep turning over like one does when it has been kept too long out of the water. Further a fish's ears lack the equipment necessary for the appreciation of *pitch,* so that what sound he does hear is simply sound, and there is not even provision for amplification. And yet a fish's " hearing " is infinitely more acute than ours and is probably more acute even than we can conceive of: it is said that a fish can " hear " a nymph often before he can see it.

A fish " hears " or more correctly detects vibrations, through its lateral line: this is a fluid-filled tube which runs the length of the fish on either side, excepting the head and the tail, which is connected to the surface by a series of capilliaries terminating in pores; the tube is lined with fibrous nerve endings which have access to the brain *via* a main nerve running parallel to the lateral line. Every movement of water, every vibration of or through the water, every alteration in the pressure of the water, is thereby communicated direct to the brain, no doubt with the appropriate indications of direction and range.

Since sound is vibration there is a much firmer contact between its origin and its reception under water than in air: humans tend to think of the underwater world as a silent one, though actually it is probably relatively far noisier than our own (excepting the intrusion of man and his machinery), and this is probably just as well for if it really were a silent world our own clumsy attempts at stealth at the waterside would have little chance of being absorbed, as in moderation they actually are, in the general din. Nevertheless if he is paying attention—that is to say if he is alert or has been alerted by something else which may worry him— a fish can certainly hear a fly and leader fall onto the surface (to say nothing of the line) even if not directly overhead, and he can also hear them being removed again.

Hit the water with the palm of your hand and from underneath it will sound like an explosion; a delicately laid line will have all the delicacy of a six-inch hawser, heard from below, and if it is recovered smartly will sound like a whip-crack: fortunately all these sounds are for the most part in competition with other similar ones of natural origin. It is not the sound of a stamping foot on the bank that a fish hears but its vibrations through earth and water that he feels; sounds originated in the air are no worry to him; thus an angler may shout and sing or, if he feels the inclination, discharge firearms; but he should not dance.

TASTE AND SMELL

Although, unlike in humans, the nostrils of a fish do not have direct access to the mouth and so result in a confusing mix-up of taste and smell, a fish is likely to be even less able to distinguish between the signals originated by these respective senses, and any difference there is must surely be academic: a fish's sense of taste and smell is again of an acuity almost incomprehensible to the human mind. Fortunately for the angler, unlike sound, taste and smell can only be brought to a fish from upstream: it is said that fish can detect the presence of an otter a great distance upstream of them and I once read an interesting article about a semi-controlled experiment with anglers' waders, which concluded that fish could be put down by their smell coming from upstream. In the positive sense I believe that a fish's ability to smell and taste are of more importance to the bait- than to the fly-fisherman; but negatively—the way in which fish can be repelled as compared to attracted—I am sure that it is of equal significance to both. Possible downstream emanations from waders have already been mentioned; here I would suggest that not only the smell of rubber is involved, but much more likely the smell of where the waders have been, notably that of petrol and associated automobile odours acquired in the boot of the car and the garage.

There is also the question of contaminated fingers handling a fly, particularly a wet fly, and if this sounds trifling I assure you that it is not: if there is a smell on a fly then a fish downstream of it will pick up that smell, and if it happens to be a smell transferred from nicotine-impregnated finger tips, or fumes from a cigarette lighter, or antiseptic, or moth-balls or any other substance inimical to an underwater creature, then a fish approaching it with his mouth open is likely at best to refuse and at worst to panic. Whether the converse is valid leads one to speculate on an interesting avenue for research; would it be advantageous, for instance, to anoint a fly with " oil of stonefly " or " essence of sedge pupa "? One thing *is* certain, however, and that is that it is certainly not disadvantageous to start fishing with clean and odourless hands, and in the case of wet flies to give them a good preliminary infusion of subaquatic mud.

THE RELATIVE IMPORTANCE OF A FISH'S SENSES

Having considered separately the five senses of a fish about which we are aware (and recognised the probable existence of a sixth about which we are not), it may not be unprofitable to think about the possible importance of each, relative to the others, *from the fish's point of view.*

The fact that infinitely more space has been devoted here to sight than to the other senses combined is merely because it is that sense in a fish which is of most significance to a fly fisherman, and because sight is the primary sense of *homo sapiens*: my own view is that it is the least important sense to a fish (and to most other animals with the exception of birds) and is certainly less vital to survival than those senses dependent on the lateral line. I had until recently an old dog (among whose many endearing features was a coat of authentic Dogsbody colour) who became totally blind; yet few humans realised this unless told about it since he managed so normally on his other senses; he moved with confidence within a quarter mile radius of my home, and this included countryside and woodland in one direction and a busy urban road in the other which he was accustomed to cross regularly and safely; he never bumped into anything that was in its proper place and found any food that was about unerringly: even away from home he could keep out of trouble, being always aware of an obstruction whether it was a brick wall or a hole in the ground, and when faced with a void in front of him would know instinctively whether it was a cliff or a shallow step down which he could jump—he even knew how far to jump. People would describe this as " marvellous " or " fantastic ", but I don't think so; I think that he would have been far more gravely disabled had he lost his sense of smell or hearing. Reports of long-surviving blind fish are not uncommon, even of blind trout, and was not the study of wild fish made elusive by their different element I have no doubt that we would hear of many more. A normal dog's sight is not as good as a man's, and the best we can claim for a fish's is that it is no better; and yet our sight is our best developed sense and the evolutionary processes towards civilisation—wearing clothes, security, the lack of the need to hunt for our food, implements, spices and tobacco, to name but a few of the factors involved—have left our other senses no more than crude shadows of those of animals, and this fact we must keep very much to the forefront of our attempts to think like a fish does.

The remaining senses of fish can be brought together into two separate groups—taste with smell and hearing with feeling—since the pairs in each group so blend with each other as to make each group into a single important sense, and I think that we can say that either of these is more important than is sight, and that hearing/feeling is the most indispensable of all. The infinitely sensitive lateral line is capable of detecting any movement from any direction; we know that it is a fish's first line of defence and also its early warning system; often enough I have no doubt that what a fish sees is merely a confirmation of what it has already heard. It is not far-fetched to speculate on the possibility that the lateral line may incorporate some system akin to radar; fish are certainly able to judge sidelong distance to a nicety—witness how a close packed shoal can turn as one fish without one touching another. It must also be the lateral line which tells them what the weather is going to do (by barometric pressure), and it is reasonably certain that a fish can find food on hearing/feeling alone.

Taste/smell must be the prime factor in food finding, by which I mean not only locating but also detecting; one can visualise appetising odours wafted in the current in much the same way as to the Bisto Kids in the advertisement, and we must remember that possibly nine-tenths of a trout's or grayling's food is picked up off the bottom, no matter how free rising they are. Taste/smell is also highly developed selectively (why else should fish accept greedily one sex of an insect species and reject the other?), and it is undoubtedly the sense mainly responsible for implementing the instinct for attaining the properly balanced diet upon which the well being of the fish depends. Finally taste/smell makes its own contribution to security, providing a sensitive warning system of potential predation both from animals and man.

In consequence of my emphasis on the acuteness of the senses of fish it may be wondered how we are able to catch them at all, and the reason is that a fish's brain is not adequate effectively to make the best use of the information continuously fed into it: if a fish had only a fraction of the brainpower of a man, that fish would be uncatchable. As it is a fish's brain can be thought of as a swtichboard for converting signals into mindless reactions; it is incapable of analysing or weighing the signals except in terms of intensity—it can differentiate between, for example, uneasiness or downright " fear "—: it is incapable of reasoning or of making a choice of reactions to a given stimulus, and a fish's reaction to a stimulus—any stimulus—is probably little different from that which can cause a man to blink his eyes (often without knowing it) when he feels instinctively that something might hit him in the face. There is obviously some capacity for memory, for a pricked fish is not so easily pricked the second time, but I doubt if the memory of a series of prickings could survive through the close season.

THE SCALES OF SURVIVAL

The interreaction of a fish's instincts may be thought of as analogous to a pair of scales; the fulcrum is " survival ", not only of the individual fish but of its species, which depends for its equilibrium upon the balancing of two factors only, " sustenance " and " security ", or more simply " food " and " fear " · there is no other ingredient, for even the spawning instinct falls under " security " and everything a fish does or feels comes under one of these headings. " Food " speaks for itself, but under fear will be included every gradation of apprehension and discomfort, including oxygen discomfort, which if not reacted to may progress towards a point where survival is at risk. Even a fish's aggression classifies itself under " fear " if it is in defence of territory, or under " food " if it is triggered by the instinct of predation.

The balance of these scales is in a state of almost continued adjustment, depending on the stimuli being received: if a hungry fish is engrossed in a fortuitous hatch of fly the " food " side of his balance will be heavily weighted so that the " fear " side will be at a discount; he will be less wary, easier to approach and easier to catch. If on the other hand something is signalled of sufficient intensity from the fear side to cause him apprehension, he will cease to feed and give his attention to survival for a while; if further fear stimuli come he may go down, or flee, according to their intensity; if not he will forget them, and the balance will again move in favour of sustenance.

If the balance is in counterpoise—if our fish is neither fearful nor hungry—he may be almost as difficult to tempt as if he were nervous; perhaps this might be an occasion for trying to stimulate his aggression by using a " flasher " type of fly to suggest a small fish.

What does happen in a fish's brain when he is made aware of the approach of a natural fly on the surface? No one knows, of course, though it is probably no more than the pressing of a button —either " take it " or " leave it ". What it most certainly is not is " here is something which I fancy to eat; having assured myself that it is safe to do so I will eat it." The advent of such a fly is probably signalled to a fish by more than one of his senses : he will see it, but if it is anything but quiescent—if it is vibrating its wings, for example—he may well have felt it first; if he is lying near the surface he may also have smelt it; nothing about it will have activated a fear button and if it is desirable he will automatically take it.

The approach of an artificial fly is not so simply dealt with; apart from there not being the " here is something I fancy to eat " routine, neither will there be " here is something which is not behaving naturally, it may be a trap so I will go down." An artificial fly has the double disadvantage not only of attracting only through the visual sense, but also of risking a give-away through all three senses : if it is dragging it will not only be seen to drag but may also be felt, and it may in addition be pushing along an inimical taste in front of it. With an artificial fly therefore there is the ever present risk of a fear and not a food reaction being set off.

It is for the angler to take a hand in the balancing of the scales —to cater for the sustenance and to take care that nothing untoward is loaded onto the security side.

COMFORT

" Comfort " to a fish has not such different connotations as when for instance, it is applied to ourselves, since for both it really means absence of hardship; freedom from fear, a full belly and ease of breathing would come high on both lists, as would (in sensible beings) absence of the necessity for undue effort : the only thing on which we really diverge is temperature, but since we are in different elements this is hardly surprising.

To a fish temperature and barometric pressure are pretty basic factors since on both depend his most basic requirement of all (and ours)—his supply of oxygen—when this is not right he will be uncomfortable and not disposed to feed. Trout, and to an even greater extent grayling, require more oxygen than possibly any other fresh water fish, and this is why they thrive only in the cleanest and least polluted waters: non-toxic pollution brings with it its Biological Oxygen Demand which mops up all available oxygen in the process of breaking up the polluting substances.

It is hardly necessary to say that a fish gets his oxygen direct from the water: he draws in water continuously through his mouth, passes it over his gills and expells it through his gill flaps; as it passes over the gills the oxygen is extracted, and how much can be extracted depends on how much is present in the water: usually the state of a fish's oxygen comfort can be gauged by the speed at which his gills are working. The proportion of oxygen in solution is governed primarily by temperature and barometric pressure, but agitated water has a better opportunity of acquiring extra oxygen than when it is smooth. The warmer water is, the less is its ability to absorb and retain oxygen, so that it follows that fish, and especially grayling and trout in that order, prefer colder water: this is why during the colder months they can be looked for in slower water where their oxygen comfort is right and less physical effort is required in holding position; when the water begins to get warmer and its oxygen content lower they are compelled to move into a faster stream because its turbulence is gathering in additional oxygen from the air, and broadly speaking the higher the water temperature the faster the water in which the fish should be looked for.

Barometric pressure is the second important factor governing oxygen supply, and here we come back into concert with the fish, for both our species thrive on high pressure which to us betokens fine weather: for the fish, however, apart from better surface feeding, it means more oxygen, since the greater weight of the atmosphere above them simply forces more oxygen into the water and keeps it there. Low atmospheric pressure naturally has the reverse effect, and this is undoubtedly the basis for the belief that thunder puts fish down; however I believe that it is not the thunder but the low pressure associated with it which can put fish off the feed because their oxygen comfort is being disturbed.

Thunder in the distance need not affect one's own fish unless their pressure is affected by it—or unless it is coming their way, in which case they will know about it long before you hear it. Even then thunder overhead need not be the spoiler it is sometimes held to be, unless its influence is sufficient to unbalance the oxygen comfort: if there is enough oxygen and to spare already in the water, due to coolness and a well broken surface, it could have little effect; if it is accompanied by a cloudburst nothing could be more efficacious in putting oxygen back in.

In attempting to assess the probable location of a fish, food supplies apart, it is necessary therefore first to weigh the factors affecting oxygen comfort; no sensible fish is going to stem a current any stronger than his instinct tells him that he needs to. Here we must make a reservation in the case of the quiet pocket in the middle of and usually under the turbulence: its existence can only be learned of by experience and normal reading of the water cannot be expected to detect it, though its possibility must always be allowed for.

If the water is warm and the atmospheric pressure low, fish must be looked for in the more violent water and even then are not likely to be over-amenable to feeding: in such a circumstance if a cooler, spring fed side stream is known of, it might be worthwhile investigating the area downstream of its confluence. Warm water and high pressure offer a little more hope though the temperature is likely to be the overriding factor, and as soon as that is reduced a situation is approached when the fish can find oxygen comfort in a more moderate current, and can think of other things, such as food. In this way one will permutate temperature with pressure and current, and with experience one should eventually be able to judge where a fish should be under the prevailing conditions: provided that the position indicated by this assessment coincides with the optimum food supply the fish ought to be there; if they are not, consideration should be given to the possibility of their having been affected by one of the other factors, for example fear.

FEAR

If I make the proposition that fear is to the mind as pain is to the body I am perhaps over-simplifying; nevertheless both sensations are built in to all creatures by nature solely as an aid to survival. Without pain we would often be scalded in our baths and walk about with broken bones or other physical damage without realising it; without fear even more of us than at present would kill ourselves in our motor cars or walk happily into the jaws of wild beasts, and a species—or individual—characterised by its lack of fear and high tolerance of pain is a more likely candidate for extinction than one which is timorous or very sensitive to pain.

However anyone who imagines that to a fish either sensation is in any way similar (except in effect) to its equivalent in a human being is guilty of that anthropomorphism to which I referred earlier: the difference is that to a fish the sense of fear comes in two stages only, cause and effect; to us it is in three stages, cause, realisation and understanding, and effect. A fish has not the capacity to interpret either sensation, but only instinctively to react; he does not feel pain as we know it or experience fear as we do, but simply reacts to yet another stimulus.

Fear in a fish, as we have already said, may be taken to mean every degree of apprehension from momentary concern to downright panic: a feeding fish may register a signal which, while alerting him, causes him merely to suspend feeding and give his attention to the security sector for a while; if no further fear signal is received he will forget it and resume feeding. Such an original signal might be engendered by the passing of a bird overhead or the falling of a twig into the water nearby; instinct may reassure him that the signals were of harmless natural origin, but not if the bird looked like a predator or the twig was dislodged by a possible predator. Fish do seem to be able to distinguish between harmless and ominous fear signals: a cow walking along the river bank will cause little concern, and it has been suggested that an angler who shambles along at the same speed as a cow might get away with it as easily; I can only assume that my own attempts at impersonation of a cow on various experimental occasions were not sufficiently lifelike; possibly two anglers moving in concert in the attitude of a pantomime cow might have more success!

Factors which spell fear to a fish, real or illusory, are too many for an attempt to be made to list them, and not by any means all are initiated by the angler: the imminence of a natural predator, be it bird, mammal or fish (pike fortunately are rare in Border waters but there are always cannibal trout) is likely to be apparent to the fish though the angler may be quite oblivious.

There are many factors concerned with fear in fish which are extremely difficult to interpret or rationalise: there is fear which is manifest but unexplainable; there is absence of fear when it should be manifest, and there is fear which only manifests itself after the cause is arrested. Taking these one at a time, let us first look at fear which is clearly recognisable in a fish but for which there is no apparent reason: every angler must have experienced the situation when he arrives at his river and finds every fish in it on tenterhooks; not just in odd pools, but uniformly along the whole stretch, fish where they can be seen, will be poised for flight with that jittery finning movement which is characteristic of an alarmed fish, and flight they will take to the moment an attempt is made to cast to them. Discounting the possibility that an inept angler has waded up the stream only a few minutes previously, we are left with only two theoretical lines of approach: the first is, since the whole water seems to be affected, that the origin of the fear is waterborne and that possibly an otter is in the water somewhere upstream; or perhaps a mild pollution has taken place, such as disinfectant swilled from a cowhouse floor (although this could be a regular occurrence) or the first rain has drained off a newly surfaced or oily road. The other possibility is that the fish have sensed an impending sharp change in atmospheric pressure, and since this could have an effect on their oxygen comfort the alarm bells have rung: whatever the source of fear the effect is likely to be the same to a fish, who as we have explained is unable to interpret his stimuli.

Absence of fear when there is every good reason for its manifestation is another tantalizing and quite frequently encountered puzzle. Examples are common, but one which comes to my mind is when I was walking a Shropshire stream with some friends to discuss possible ways of river improvement; we had no thought of fishing, in fact the occasion was just after the trout season had closed. At one point we were concerned with concentrating the flow, and it was suggested that a croy placed in a certain way would have the desired effect, so to test the theory we there and then began to construct an experimental croy utilising large stones from the river bed; there was much upheaval and banging and splashing, enough to send every fish within a quarter mile either way scurrying in terror, but in the middle of it all two trout started to rise in the turbid water not more than four yards downstream of us, to the nymphs we were displacing. I do not propose to strain the reader's credulity by suggesting that those fish sensed that our presence and activities were not malevolent towards them, but what explanation is there? Apparently the scales had come down so heavily on the food side as to outweigh entirely what should have been a veritable blanket of fear signals! This is by no means the only time that I have been made aware of fishes' attitude to me, rodless in the close season, compared with an armed approach at other times. Can this sort of thing really be regarded as evidence of the existence of a sixth sense which is beyond our comprehension? Or on this occasion did we really manage to get ourselves registered as cows trampling in the water— for the sight of fish rising among cows doing just that is something most fishermen have seen.

The third example concerns a fish already uneasy who, nevertheless, maintains his position until the signals which (presumably) occasioned his discomfort cease, and then he panics. My own experience of this happening is when I have come up too close to a fish which I didn't realise was there, and having glimpsed him in the water have frozen: if my approach has been behind his shoulder he will not have seen me, but will almost certainly have felt my footsteps albeit they were stealthy; for a second or so after my freezing he will remain, exhibiting increasing agitation, and then he will go like an arrow. There is no doubt in my mind that such a fish is activated by the cutting off completely of signals which in the first instance were merely cautionary, and this seems to indicate an additional built-in device which requires a release from fear signals already registered. Who knows?—the angler's best recourse in such a situation might be to go on quietly marking time!

THE RECOVERY FROM FEAR

An understanding of the time it takes for fish to recover completely from the effects of fear stimuli is important to the angler's deployment of his effort and usually limited time: in other words, how soon can he return to a good fish which he has put down with the best chance of catching it? A rule of thumb which I have often seen quoted is twenty minutes per pound weight, but to me this is meaningless since it ignores the fact that fear signals which put down fish are received in varying intensity, and are thus subject to varying recovery times: it further ignores the fact that a fish alerted but not actually put down still needs to be rested, and also that recovery time is likely to vary widely between waters depending on the stock (stew-bred or wild) and their degree of education. Fear stimuli may cause a fish briefly to stop feeding; to increase his vigilance; to become agitated; to drift into deeper water or under overhanging cover; or to bolt with varying degrees of panic, and the time taken to recover from any of these stages is likely to be in proportion to the intensity of the activating signal.

An ability to judge recovery time is of especial value to the Border angler because situations are often met with where it is necessary to disturb fish in order to get oneself into a position to cast to them at all; the regular Border fly fisherman will know exactly what I mean, though it is very difficult to explain: because of aggravated drag or lack of casting room, in order to position one's self to cast to a certain lie it is necessary first to wade or crawl or slide in a way which must cause some disturbance to the fish, or to other fish who will disturb *your* fish; having gained the desired position you must sit quietly and take an interest in all that is going on in and around the river, and perhaps smoke your pipe until it is judged that the fish have forgotten about you. This is not too hard if the fish can be seen or if its rise-forms are to be seen, in which case it is necessary only to wait until regular feeding has been resumed. If, more likely, the fish cannot be seen and is thought to be feeding on mid-water nymphs, then all the time that can be spared should be allowed, and a bit more beside; even then one has to face the possibility of being wrong both about the time and the feeding. Such places are often skipped by what I call the " greyhound " type of fisherman, who likes to cover a couple of miles of river before lunch, but for that reason among others I favour them as likely haunts of good fish as well as promoting the contemplative side of the sport.

In the same context it is a fact that I have caught more fish, often from a sitting position, having rested for ten minutes before commencing to fish a pool, than ever I have done by starting to fish immediately upon my arrival at its tail: I think that the reason for this is not only that the fish have been given time to settle down again after having perhaps received cautionary stimuli, though this is likely to be the most important, but also because a detailed if unconscious appreciation of the water is made during the resting period. Often a quite different approach will be made as a result of those few minutes' contemplation from what would have been done had one moved straight in, and more often still fish will be seen to rise during the interval of observation who would not otherwise have been marked at all.

HOLTING PLACES

A final factor concerned with fear in relation to watercraft is where a fish will go when frightened. All except the smallest trout have a fixed holting place; for a smaller trout this may be communal and perhaps not particularly secure, but as he grows in stature and seniority he will progressively acquire better and safer holting places, and one factor in the location of his holt will be its availability to his feeding station, and *vice-versa*. Grayling being shoal fish do not holt in the same way except for large old fish who have become solitary; the majority select their feeding places in relation to the deepest pools, to the depths of which they can slip when alarmed.

On Border streams holting places for either species are not so freely available as on large rivers or chalk streams (on the latter there are often continuous runs of overhung bank which can be regarded as continuous holting places, to say nothing of dense weed-beds). In general a section through a typical Border stream will reveal a perhaps gravelly shallow on one side deepening to the base of a clean cut and almost vertical scour on the other, in neither of which, without the intervention of other features, are good holting places likely. There *are* undercut banks, of course, often in conjunction with rocks and larger stones, but the majority of good Border holts are found in association with tree roots; here underwater cavities can be found whose depth and impregnability are amazing and often unsuspected, and these are the places which the better trout like to have adjacent to their feeding stations. Since, as we shall see shortly, good feeding stations also have an affinity to tree roots, there is here a reciprocity which should never be overlooked.

In attempting to assess the probable positions of better fish, possible holting places are an important consideration; while a likely holting area does not necessarily betoken a good fish a stretch of water patently devoid of such places would offer little hope of containing worthwhile specimens in spite of other features being favourable.

One factor which should not be lost sight of is the possibility of an intermediate holt: where circumstances place a good feeding station rather farther from his holt than a fish finds comfortable, he may have a place somewhere in between, not so secure as his main holt, to which he can repair if merely alarmed, reserving his main holt for when he is really frightened and, of course, for longer resting periods.

AVAILABILITY OF FOOD

In the context of watercraft and striving to think like a fish, food is one of the most important elements, if not *the* most important: if there were no food there would be no fish and conversely where the best feeding is there also are the best fish. The individual items on the fish's menu are dealt with elsewhere, and this leaves us free here to consider where the fish will find the best feeding in exchange for the least effort; the latter requirement—minimal effort—is a significant factor in its own right; we have pointed out, perhaps facetiously, that no sensible fish will expend any more effort than he feels compelled to, but this is not the result of an endemic laziness but a requirement of metabolism.

The food which a fish obtains provides him with energy, but he has to expend energy to obtain food; if he uses up more energy in rising to a fly than he will get back as a result of digesting it he is on a clear loser, and if he goes on doing it he will gradually fade away: on the other hand if he shows a profit on each transaction—if every fly risen to provides more energy than is burnt up in securing it—there is a margin which can be devoted to other vital purposes, such as necessary bodily functions, the maintenance and replacement of tissue, growth, and provision for flight. Instinct, therefore, causes fish, like most wild creatures, to secure their food with the optimum of economy and to strike a balance which will secure them the best return.

THE FOOD LANE

On every watercourse, from the smallest brook to the largest river there is something which I have always called the " food lane " or the " main food lane ". On Border streams there is generally only one food lane, though occasionally it will divide, but on bigger rivers there may be several but even then one of them is dominant. The food lane is the path down which nine-tenths of the trash of the stream, floating and not-quite-floating, is carried —nothing large (for bigger objects find their own paths down-stream, but even so they spend much of their journey in the food lane)—but all the small rubbish that rains down continuously upon the surface of a river; bits of twig and bark, flower petals and seeds of grasses, leaves and pollens; and among the trash will be found something much more valuable.

What creates the food lane? It generally follows the line of the fastest current, but this really implies the least impeded current; by this I mean that it is possible for there to be a faster current elsewhere that may be hindered by a shallow stony bottom and become broken; in such a case the food lane will tend to choose a course of greater depth and smoother surface, if such exists, which could be slightly slower. Just as the water cloven by the bow of a ship folds in again behind its stern, so that of slower currents is drawn toward an adjacent swifter one, and with it is also drawn what it carries on or in—or just beneath—its surface : thus there is a continuous movement of surface trash towards a point where both sides exert an equalising pressure upon each other, and there we have the line of the food lane. Sometimes, especially in early spring when there is little rubbish falling on the water, the food lane is difficult to see except perhaps for odd bubbles, and its route must be divined : in high summer and autumn there is usually no mistaking it and it can sometimes be found to be em-barrassingly overloaded with detritus.

Into this focal point is drawn also the rack of insect lives, the dead, the dying and the doomed; and not only these, for the same influences which draw the ruined insects into the lane bring also many of those newly-hatched flies who have yet to assert their in-dependence of the current. It will thus be seen that from a fish's point of view the food lane is well named.

Trout will not normally lie under the food lane unless its current is moderate or they have a pocket of quiet water to lie in, for example behind a submerged stone; grayling will, but usually in places where the depth suggests that the current on the bottom is diffused and less violent than at the surface. Where the food lane is moving rapidly trout will tend to lie in the quieter currents to the side of it, but always so placed that they can keep an eye on what is coming along.

Although the influences which determine the placing of the food lane are likely to affect also what happens just under the surface, perhaps for some distance, it would be quite wrong to assume that the same situation obtains all the way down and that wherever the visible food lane is, there is also an invisible food lane extending vertically downward from it. On the contrary, once you are six inches or so beneath the surface a different set of rules starts to apply, because while surface currents are confined within two dimensions those below can expand into a third—height, or if you will, depth. It is quite possible, therefore, though not I think common, for the underwater food lane to be in quite a different part of the stream from the surface one. Nevertheless it is rarely likely to be following exactly the same course as the surface lane nor will it normally be anything like so concentrated, since because of its extra elbow-room it can be relatively diffused. It follows that an unthinking angler could be presenting his dry fly immaculately in the food lane while the worthwhile fish are feeding on nymphs in another part of the stream entirely. Although, therefore, the food lane is by definition the visible surface food lane, the existence of its invisible subaquatic counterpart must not be lost sight of.

The factors which govern the placing of the line of the food lane are identical with those which determine the set of the current in the same place: if we visualise an imaginary (thank Heaven!) river which runs in a dead straight line and has smooth vertical sides and a level unencumbered bottom, it will be difficult to identify any sort of food lane since the current will be flowing so evenly, but what there is of it is likely to be straight down the centre, the influences being the frictional retarding effect of the sides and bottom. If, however, we place one stone or one branch in the water at one side of the river, its even flow will immediately be disrupted for some distance downstream; the water striking our small obstruction will be deflected outward, shouldering as its goes the water which was running alongside it and initiating a diminishing chain reaction right across the stream, and dislocating in its progress the original straight axis of the food lane. Eventually striking the far bank our disruptive influence, if it is still strong enough, will deflect again, once more displacing the food lane—and so on, until it is spent.

A normal river, especially a turbulent Border stream, has thousands of deflecting obstructions in every mile, not only at the sides but on the bottom as well; these normally work against each other sending the set of the current from side to side and up and down; sometimes two such obstructions work in unison, balancing their opposition, and then the river is forced narrowly between them, forming a swift deep glide. The food lane is generally to be looked for over the swiftest and deepest part, following the set of the current first on one side and then the other, and occasionally down the middle; on bends it usually follows round near the extreme outside, underneath the cliff-like scour, unless there is some obstruction inside the circumference which will deflect it inward.

Most typical Border streams comprise a series of pools, the upper and lower limits of each of which are clearly defined to the angler, although the layman possibly sees only a continuous stretch of running water: of course there are plenty of places where the levelness of the land permits the river to maintain a levelness of surface and bed for sufficiently long to justify the term " stretch " rather than " pool ", and this can also be applied to places where an obstacle, sometimes natural but often man made, such as a weir, causes the water to back up for a considerable distance and produce what we often refer to as a " canal stretch ". There are also lengths where the gradient of the land is such that the stream is not able to form pools, and trundles for some way down a " stickle "—a stretch of shallow broken water in which only smaller fish are likely to be found. But in general, I repeat, a Border river is a series of pools, and each pool will have a neck (through which most of the water enters) and a tail (through which it leaves) although the width of the surface across the points where the neck and the tail are located can be the same as across the body of the pool. Alternatively the water may enter or leave a pool (or both), relatively evenly across the bed, so that the pool is only defined by its up- and down-stream

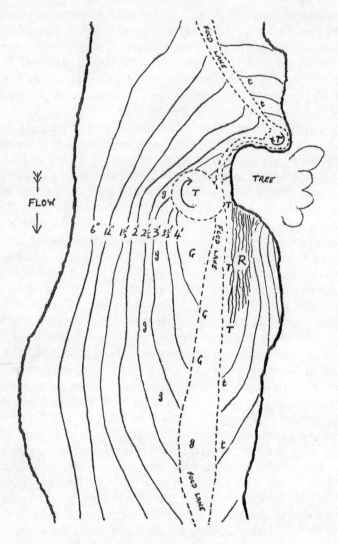

THE GEOGRAPHY OF A TYPICAL BORDER POOL

t : likely positions of trout.
T :   „   „   „ good trout.
g :   „   „   „ grayling.
G :   „   „   „ good grayling.
R : submerged roots.

shallowing, and in this case the locations of the neck and the tail can be determined by the food lane, which will pass through both.

Border pools come in all shapes and sizes, but generally speaking their length does not exceed two or three times their width, since by that time the contour of the land will have demanded that the water finds itself a lower level, and out it will go through the tail which, unless there is an intervening stickle, becomes the neck of the pool below.

A TYPICAL BORDER POOL

One of the commonest types of Border pool (I can think of literally dozens like it) has its neck in association with a projecting tree root; the main current comes in through the neck, perhaps at an angle, to strike the bank immediately upstream of the tree, where it forms a pocket in which a raft of small debris is trapped, perhaps revolving slowly, being augmented continuously from upstream while at the same time detaching a regular trickle of earlier-arrived trash into the downstream food lane; the pocket is often of considerable depth because of the scour, and is likely to harbour at least one good trout, who is taking advantage of the raft both for its cover and its pickings, of the nearness of the undercut root for its holt, and the fact that this is one of the most difficult lies of the river to cast a fly to. After passing round the pocket the current is forced outward round the up-stream edge of the projecting root until, jostled by water which has bypassed the pocket, it is free to flow downstream again and loses a little of the force it received in being squeezed round the knuckle of the root. The above-surface part of the root here gives way (if the tree is a willow or an alder, and it usually is) to a submerged mat of trailing aquatic roots: this is the deepest part of the pool and trout are likely to be lying parallel to the trailing roots with the better fish probably placed opposite to where the roots begin to thin out, above a point where the bottom commences to rise again. If grayling are present they are likely to be either behind and deeper than the better trout—on the bottom but beneath the food lane—, or away to the side on the steep shoulder of the pool opposite the trailing roots, ignoring the food lane and concentrating on nymphs.

However while trout will take up a fixed feeding station having regard to the factors which will make it the most desirable each can aspire to, grayling, except in the swiftest current, will wander: although in groups they will follow individual circuits which, on the rare occasions they can be observed, are predictable, since they tend always to follow the same route. In the pool I have described I would expect the grayling to move in a semi-circle parallel to the contour of the outer and downstream upward shelving of the pool, the lower end of the " beat " being its inter-section with the food lane and the upper end opposite the knuckle of the root; always keeping close to the steeply sloping shoulder of the pool they will work upstream at one level and then drift down at another, which could be above or below the first.

The food lane will be seen to have entered the pool by the neck, taken a few turns round the pocket, travelled outwards with the current round the knuckle of the root and then taken the easiest course to the tail, its progress running parallel to the trail-ing underwater roots; it will vary in width, being narrow where the current is concentrated, but more dispersed in those places where the current itself has more space to spread itself and moder-ate its flow.

WHERE TO LOOK FOR FISH

It will be seen that fish are most likely to be found in those places where some or all of the factors we have discussed combine to their optimum advantage. Food being the governing factor, they will seek the best position for locating and obtaining it subject to satisfactory conditions of oxygen comfort, safety from molestation including facilities for early warning, and easily achieved and secure refuge and minimal physical effort.

With these considerations in mind, where specifically on a Border stream would we expect to find a fish? The raft of debris in the root-pocket we have already discussed, but similar rafts are to be found in other places, notably where the food lane passes under twigs or branches hanging in the water. These rafts have in common not only the potential of a better than average fish, but by the nature of their location the fact that presentation to them usually has to be made at least square across, and frequently actually downstream, a task often best delegated to a nymph.

The situation where the decellerating food lane runs parallel and close to submerged roots can be looked for in many circumstances other than those described, and any vertical bank which holds a promise of underwater hiding places and has the food lane adjacent is worthy of attention. Any projection into the stream, by virtue of the way it causes the current to concentrate downstream of its tip, will create its own brief food lane even if it does not obtrude into the food lane proper, and fish should always be looked for below such projections.

Another fruitful place is immediately downstream of a trailing weed bed; weed in Border streams is more often than not river crowfoot, a Ranunculus species; we don't have much of it but what we have we treasure. The weed harbours a flourishing population of nymphs and other aquatic creatures, and whenever one looses its footing what better place to lie and wait for it than the tail of the weed bed? There a fish can watch both sides at once and be only a flick of its tail from the safety of the bed itself. Where a weed bed is associated with a stony but otherwise fairly level and shallow bottom it may extend right across the stream and be channelled in several places; each channel then becomes a food lane in its own right, but it is not usually difficult to select the main one, although all may repay searching: the difficulty is in persuading a fly for any distance down such a narrow strip without instant drag—especially with a dry fly—and this is one of the few instances when a cast from directly downstream, or nearly so, is justified. Obviously the search should be made from the bottom upwards so that only places already searched are lined.

Generalisations are often made about fish lying behind stones, the inference being that wherever a stone is seen sticking up out of the water there will *ipso facto* be a fish behind it; but this is not so, and much will depend on the size and the shape of the stone. If the stone is shaped like a ship—longer than it is wide and with sharp ends up- and down-stream—it will not be very attractive for a fish to lie behind, because the water will close round it with no lessening of speed and increased turbulence. What the fish is seeking is a quiet and restful haven just out of the main current, and any obstruction of the right size and shape, not necessarily a stone, can provide it; this presupposes a fair width and blunt ends so that the water once parted will stay parted for a short distance and leave a quiet backwater in the lee of the obstruction. My own observation seems to show that in general fish prefer to lie behind wholly submerged stones rather than those which are emergent, but there is nothing hard or fast about this.

Areas of quiet water are often to be found just upstream of the merging of two currents: the main stream may have been divided by a rising central bed or even an emergent island, and the currents come together again in much the same way as when divided by a rock, only on a larger scale, leaving a triangular calm patch which almost always harbours fish. Such quiet triangles are often easily recognised, but when their presence is not obvious it should nevertheless be assumed in the circumstances I have described.

Trout, particularly, like to lie under overhanging objects such as drooping branches: doubtless cover and the possibility of falling food have something to do with this, but I also get the impression that fish like to locate themselves on a feature, inside or out of their environment, even when no obvious tactical advantage is apparent. This may be something akin to the instinct in a man who, in a featureless place will put down his load and rest himself near the largest stone he can see, although it is only fractionally larger than all the others. Fish are thus more likely to be seen opposite the up- and down-stream edges of bridges, under overhanging branches, or placed square of prominent underwater features. Similarly fish dislike featureless expanses of bottom, no doubt because they are more easily seen over it, and given a choice will always lie over gravel which offers both trout and grayling a good background camouflage. Both species of fish have an obvious preference for a stream bed which is sloping upward towards downstream, though grayling also favour a fairly abrupt upward slope to the side. This surely has something to do with the narrowing upward of the underwater food lane and also an instinct for protection from attack from beneath. Grayling very rarely expose their bellies to an approach from this direction and even trout never seem too comfortable if they have a large area of open water underneath them. Certainly if there must be a rule-of-thumb regarding fishes' preferences in bottom conditions, it is that both trout and grayling will always elect if possible to lie over a rising gravelly bed.

Chapter Six

ON FLY DRESSING

MANY PEOPLE, without giving it much thought, refer to " fly tying ", and in doing so I think that they devalue both the art of
the professional and the painstaking, tongue-protruding efforts of
the amateur. Parcels are tied; fishing flies, provided that they do
not look too much like parcels, are dressed.

Every fly fisherman, especially if he aspires to being a " whole "
fisherman, should at least try his hand at dressing his own flies. I
believe that many such men, inwardly feeling that they *should* do
this, do not actually get round to starting simply because they
convince themselves in advance that fly dressing is beyond their
capability : they persuade themselves that their large and horny
hands and blunt fingers could not possibly produce an object of
such delicacy as a trout fly, but this is not so; I am sure that anyone
who is keen enough can dress a fly which is acceptable to fish in
a surprisingly short time, and especially the uncomplicated
patterns which are most successful on Border streams. The main
hurdle is in overcoming the initial doubts and inertia, and getting
a few basic requirements together to make a start.

Why should I so strongly advocate the dressing of one's own
flies? There are a number of reasons and one of them is *not*
economy. Paradoxically the lifelong fly fisher and fly dresser who
has made and fished all the patterns that he has read of or had
recommended, often reaches a point of ultimate simplicity whereat
he is dressing his deadliest flies out of materials which cost him
virtually nothing, apart from the hooks; yet before reaching this
stage he will probably have spent a small fortune on exotic
feathers and furs and fancy tinsels and the like, in quantities to
last not only his but several other lifetimes. While I now know,

therefore, that it is possible to dress one's own flies at a fraction of the cost of bought ones—that one can make all the patterns necessary from a " bargain dozen " of assorted cocks' capes for thirty shillings, a pheasant's tail, some rabbits' fur and sheeps' wool probably for nothing, not to mention contributions from domestic pets—I know that it is quite useless proffering economy as a justification for dressing one's own flies, since I also know that once the " bug " has bitten it is beyond human control to prevent the freshly converted enthusiast from going out and buying all manner of beautiful materials, and to go on doing so all the way through his enslavement.

No, the chief advantage to be derived from dressing one's own flies is that it is the only way of ensuring that they are made in the way which one wants (or more correctly in the way which the fish in one's own waters prefer), and *on the hooks which one wants.* Shop-sold flies can never be other than standard, no matter how good they are: by this I mean that they are unlikely to have been dressed with your (or for that matter any other) particular water in mind, and while they may be ideal on some waters are likely to be under- or over-dressed for the requirement of a specific fishery; this is especially so in the case of Border dry flies, where I have found the chief requirements to be relatively heavy hackling combined with an equally relatively sparse body dressing.

Many of the Border flies which I have mentioned or shall be mentioning, although well-known to the initiated and listed in the more comprehensive books, are just not to be obtained from the average tackle shop, even one specialising in game fishing: I doubt if there are half-a-dozen shops in the whole country where a request for a Dogsbody would be met with other than an uncomprehending stare, and the same applies to a lesser extent to such Border flies as the Paragon, Hereford Alder, Borderer and Ermine Moth, while I know of only one professional dresser who still produces Barrett's Bane and Professor. This position is brought about by understandable merchandising methods which only supply against a known profitable demand, and the answer for the Border fisherman is to dress his own.

Shop flies, like so many other things, can be good, bad or indifferent; in general you get what you pay for. The price of flies at the time of writing is ridiculously and (to the producer) uneconomically low, due to the intervention in the trade of a large number of " pin-money " semi-professional dressers, so that the most expensive are still very cheap—so much so that many potential self-dressers lack the spur to get started.

The purchaser of shop flies should be able to become discriminating of quality of both materials and hooks as his knowledge of these things develops, but he is not likely to find out how soon his fly will come undone until it happens. Even if he does not incline to dress his own he would be advised to learn to know his patterns and the materials of which they should be constructed : it has not been unknown for a tyro to go into a shop confidently naming a pattern and to walk out again happily believing that he had bought what he asked for; since neither he nor the shopkeeper knew what it looked like he got something else which he didn't know the name of either. Fortunately very few tackle dealers indeed are likely to take advantage of the ignorance of a beginner, but there are plenty of semi-professional fly dressers who will substitute materials either for reasons of economy or out of ignorance of the original recipe. One of the most common and glaring examples of the latter must be the confections which are regularly offered as Tup's Indispensables : it is true that for many years the ingredients for the Tup's body remained a closely guarded secret, but Courtney Williams's Dictionary[1] has been in print continuously since 1949 and in it there is a comprehensive description, so that there is absolutely no excuse for modern versions being incorrectly dressed, particularly since none of the materials is rare or expensive.

I do not want to give the impression that I am against substitution of materials as such; indeed it is something which I myself regularly practice where I find it advantageous to my own purpose. However if I dressed a fly similar to a Tup's but with a body partially composed of pink knitting wool, I would not try to pass it off as a Tup's Indispensable, especially if I were going to sell it.

The skilled amateur who only makes flies for himself and perhaps his friends has the edge over the professional in that time is not a factor with which he need be over-concerned. In terms of cost efficiency time is vital to the professional, who cannot hope to make any sort of a living unless he is capable of

---

[1] " A Dictionary of Trout Flies ". A. Courtney Williams. A. & C. Black, London.

dressing at least a dozen standard flies an hour, hour after hour—most professionals do a lot more than that—and this includes grading and preparing hackles, waxing silks and mixing dubbings, and *should* also include testing individual hooks. While a few top professionals can top this norm with ease—I know a man who can dress three dozen sophisticated trout flies per hour, each one a little gem—it will readily be seen that there is much room for inferior work, especially among semi-professionals striving to achieve an economic output, and employed dressers on piecework. The professional dresser cannot allow himself time to get the fly just right; he cannot take off or put on an extra turn of hackle or increase or diminish his dubbing, or unwind his ribbing and re-do it in closer or wider turns: again this does not signify in the case of the first class dressers, since their flies will be like peas in a pod anyway, but they are in the minority these days. The professionally dressed fly has to be put together rapidly and without pause; when it is finished if it is bad it is rejected, but the degree of badness justifying rejection is at the discretion of the operative or his or her employer. Most " factory " flies are dressed by highly skilled girls, many of whom are far more proficient than any amateur; but they are dressing to a pattern, from little heaps of materials set before them, perhaps unaware of the purpose or even the name of the fly they are dressing and probably not knowing what a trout or grayling would look like if they saw one.

While the luxury of taking one's time is one of the great advantages of dressing one's own flies, it should not be thought that the longer one takes the better the finished product will be: on the contrary too much messing about will often result in a badly- or over-dressed fly. An amateur dresser should try from the start to achieve the best speed he can, subject always to getting the fly just as he wants it, and ensuring that it will be worn out before it starts to come undone!

Dressing his own flies is one way of helping the trout fisherman to endure his close season—perhaps even as a substitute for writing books—but surely its chief aesthetic value is in the satisfaction which derives from deceiving a fish with a confection of fur and feather which he has made himself : how many of us do not remember vividly the first undersized fish which honoured us by accepting one of our own creations?

As with casting, it is not my intention here to attempt instruction in fly dressing; I shall assume that my reader already has the rudiments even if he is not already an accomplished dresser in his own right. I have already mentioned that my own early fly dressing instruction was acquired from books—I am especially indebted to Sir Gerald Burrard's[1] and among modern works I find those of Geoffrey Bucknall some of the most practical and sensible —and from the many articles and tips which appear in angling periodicals; nevertheless I aver that there is no substitute for " demonstration with explanation " and since nowadays this is so readily available to most people in the form of further education evening classes I unhesitatingly recommend it to all who propose to try their hand. My purpose here is to add a few notes of my own which may be regarded as a supplement to the formal basic instruction; some of my suggestions may be found to be at odds with standard practice, but no matter, no one is obliged to follow me; and for those who do it is always better to learn a job the conventional way before you can appreciate the advantages of modification : one can hardly sit down to dress a variant without first knowing how to dress the standard pattern.

VICE

The most important basic requirement of the fly dresser, especially the novice, is a good vice; this is not a matter for economy and the beginner is advised to buy the best one he can afford : if it is proposed to make salmon as well as trout and grayling flies, care should be taken in choosing one which will accommodate both types of hook. A good vice is one which will grip all sizes of hook firmly but without excessive force which may result in damage, and at the same time allow the fly to be worked on from all angles without obstruction and to be turned round and raised and lowered as necessary to suit the convenience of the dresser. By " good vice " I do not necessarily mean the most expensive, for the latter may have all sorts of " assisting " gadgets projecting from and around it which, once the earliest novice stage has been passed, will only get in the way. I do not think that it is of critical importance whether the vice has conventional straight jaws or is of the

---

[1] " Fly Tying, Principles & Practice ". Major Sir Gerald Burrard, Bt., D.S.O., R.F.A. Herbert Jenkins : London.

collet type; I personally incline to the former since the point of the hook can more easily be masked, thus avoiding catching and occasionally severing the silk on it, usually at a crucial juncture. There is also the consideration that the jaws of a straight-jawed vice, because of their larger holding area and more comprehensive grip on the hook, do not wear out so quickly as those of the collet type.

Fly dressing without a vice or with a so-called hand vice is not, I think something which should be contemplated by a beginner. My own view is that it should not be contemplated by anyone; where I have seen it done I regret that I have entertained the uncharitable feeling that it was a kind of " party piece ", as I would were I to watch someone dressing a fly in a vice but with one hand tied behind his back. The man who takes his fly dressing materials with him to the waterside for the purpose of " instant imitation " may believe that he is behaving like a whole fisherman in the classic mould, but I would describe him as someone who has gone fishing having made inadequate advance preparations. I believe that the proper conditions for fly dressing are indoors in a comfortable atmosphere and posture, at a stable well-lit bench and with a good vice.

HACKLE

The hackles are undoubtedly the most important part of the dressing of a dry trout or grayling fly, and it therefore behoves the novice fly dresser to learn very early on to be a judge of hackle quality. Shape and texture are both important, but we will deal with shape first: the illustrations show extremes in shape, and in practice most of our flies will be made from something in between the two: the best ones will be left to the wealthy dilettante who is more concerned with the appearance of his flies than their effect upon the fish, and the worst we will use either for whisks or clipped-hackle bodies or discard entirely. If you examine a whole hackle feather closely, starting at the butt, it will be seen that the lowest fibres are downy; those give way to fibres which while not obviously downy nevertheless have a web of short fuzz for the greater part of their length; as your examination progresses towards the tip the proportion of this web in the length of each fibre decreases until it ceases altogether and the length of the fibres decreases proportionately: on many hackle feathers, especi-

COCK HACKLES

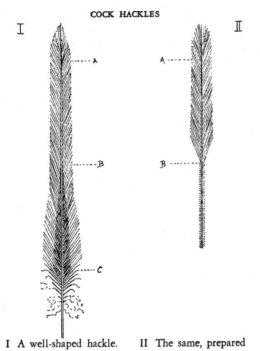

I   A well-shaped hackle.   II   The same, prepared

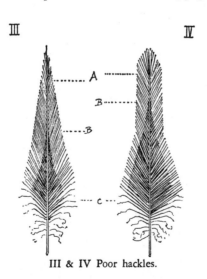

III & IV   Poor hackles.

A – B: Working areas. B – C: Webbed areas.

ally lighter coloured ones, the webbed portion can be clearly seen as a spear-shaped area of greater density. Once the apex of the webbed area is passed, and all the fibres are quite without basal down, the overall taper of the whole feather becomes noticeably less steep and in a good hackle the fibres will be of roughly even length for some distance—almost to the tip, in fact: it is this parallel portion of the hackle which we use, and no part of the webbed area should be included since a webbed fibre is substantially softer and weaker. The longer and narrower that the non-webbed portion of the feather is, therefore, the better the hackle is, subject to texture.

The fibres of a well-textured hackle should sparkle and be stiffly springy: I have seen experts bend hackles into loops and press the tips of the spread fibres against their lips; with a good hackle they can feel the tip of each fibre almost pricking them, while a poor one will feel more like a powder puff. Well-textured cock hackles are only obtained from birds at least three or four years old, and since cockerels in this country are rarely allowed to survive for more than a few months, virtually all our hackle feathers have to be imported, mostly from the Far East.

Hackle feathers are best bought by the whole neck, or cape; not only is this more economical but it is by far the best way of storing them and keeping them graded for size. Usually not more than the top third of the cape is usable for trout and grayling flies, the remainder being of value only for tail whisks or for reservoir streamer flies. The smallest feathers will be seen to come from the top of the cape, near to where the comb of the cockerel was, and get progressively larger as you move down the neck. The classic way of determining the correct size of dry fly hackle for a given hook is to choose one the fibres of which, when the feather is bent round the eye, will reach as far as the point but no further than the barb. In practice it will be found that with the hook-sizes employed in Border fishing—and indeed in most river fly fishing—if this standard is adhered to it restricts the dresser to a comparatively tiny area of the cape. My own unashamed answer to this is to clip my hackles, although I realise that in some quarters this is a solecism akin to shooting a fox. Clipped hackles on a shop-bought fly might justifiably arouse suspicion, but I am personally satisfied that the clipping of a hackle of known quality on a self-dressed fly is not only acceptable but actually advan-

tageous to the object of imitation: no insect in nature has legs
which terminate in sharp points, and any aquatic insect which was
so equipped would be unable to rest on the surface without its
feet penetrating the film. An examination of the legs of an insect
—any insect—will show that its feet are relatively large to the rest
of its leg, and certainly no thinner, as are those of most creatures.
Some successful (though possibly not top-drawer) fly fishermen of
my acquaintance go so far as to trim their hackles not with scissors
but with a cigarette-end, thus terminating each hackle fibre with
a life-like blob which rides the water (dare I say it?) just like an
insect's foot.

I would not wish this to be regarded as licence to use any old
size of hackle on a fly, but simply to make a number of extra
hackles on each neck available to the dresser: as the hackles on a
cape become progressively larger it will be noted that the space
between the fibres, where they are attached to the central stem, in-
creases: the fibres of a " size 12 " hackle can be three times as
far apart as those on a " size 18 ", so that such a hackle wound on
a small hook would require three times as many turns of a much
coarser central stem to achieve the same amount of hackling, and
this would bid farewell to any attempt at delicacy. I would not recommend the use of hackles more than two sizes larger than the
hook for which they are intended, though I feel strongly that such
hackles, clipped, will be more attractive to fish than those of the
correct size, unclipped.

A rough-and-ready way of determining if the hackles of a dry
fly are too long is to toss the fly several times onto a flat surface:
if it mostly lands in the same attitude which one would want it to
adopt on the water, then there is not a great deal wrong with it.
If, however, it persistently chooses a position wherein either its
head or its tail is in the air, then judicious use of the scissors is
indicated.

I usually find it sufficient to clip the hackles of a finished fly on
the underside only—but square across, not on a radius. This has
the effect of encouraging the fly always to land right-way up and
leaves the remaining hackle fibres, not in contact with the water
and seen more dimly by the fish, to present a softer and more
gauzy outline—more appropriate to wings—than the harder one
suggested by hackles clipped to a regular length all round.

Because the " working area "—the parallel section free of basal webbing described above—of the average fair-quality hackle is shorter than most of us would like, it is too easy in a one-hackle fly to fall into the temptation to use more of the hackle than we ought, and to allow a little of webbed portion to be included. This snare can be avoided if, as a matter of course, not less than two hackles are habitually used on a dry fly: I am always prepared to use three or even four hackles if circumstances require them, by which I mean if colour and texture are right but working areas short or if I need to mix colours to achieve a desired effect. The use of two hackles is additionally advantageous because I am personally convinced that two hackles of differing colours are more attractive than either two hackles of the same colour or a single high-quality one. Nowadays even if a standard dressing specifies one hackle colour only I will use two—one of the named colour and one of a colour which I know to be attractive or which represents some other feature of the natural insect, for instance the wings. The mixing of hackles can also be used to advantage when the precise colour called for may be rare or expensive; for example honey dun can be simulated by mixing a honey hackle with a slatey-blue one, or rusty dun by combining blue with rusty brown. The use of an additional hackle can be of advantage when the only feathers of a required colour at the disposal of the dresser are of poor quality; these can be reinforced by a further quality hackle of a different but suitable colour, thus ensuring that the fly not only embodies the correct colour but is also capable of standing on its own feet: the same applies when the dressing of a dry fly calls for hen or jackdaw hackles, partridge breast or snipe's rump or other similar soft feathers whose use alone make for a rather limp fly. Finally one of the really big advantages of the two or more hackled fly, when one of the hackles is a light-coloured one as is the case with my own sheet anchor, the Dogsbody, is the ease with which they can be seen by the angler on dappled and often shaded Border waters: this is itself far from being a new idea; it has been practised in America since the turn of the century, such flies being known there as " bi-visibles ".

Some natural colours in hackles are virtually unobtainable these days, and even when the colour can be found the actual quality of shape and texture may leave much to be desired: perhaps the best examples are the various Andalucian blue and brown duns which, on the rare occasions when they can be found, are prohibitively priced. There is a great deal of prejudice against dyed hackles (curious, since dyed body materials are readily accepted and frequently specified), but I have not personally found any difference at all, provided the hackle itself is of good quality: I have never in fact owned a good quality Andalucian cape, but I have not been aware of any exception taken by the fish to my blue hackled artificials. Except as an interesting exercise I have not found it worthwhile to dye my own feathers, since it is so very difficult to drop on the precise shading I am trying to achieve: I find it more satisfactory to go to a professional and make a choice from a selection, and thereby match my precise requirements as to both shade and quality.

For preparing hackle feathers for tying-in the standard advice seems to be that the unwanted fibres should be *stripped* from the stalk, but I do not subscribe to this. In tearing away the unwanted fibres you also remove, from either side of the stalk, a hefty strip of the surface integument which is the strongest part of the quill : when this is tied down firmly and then bent outward at an acute angle, a point of weakness is unnecessarily created. It is far better to *trim* the unwanted fibres with a pair of scissors, cutting upward from the butt, and it is surprisingly difficult accidentally to cut the quill itself: this method has the additional advantage of leaving a short stubble of the fibres to assist in the anchorage of the hackle butt.

The conventional way of tying in the hackle is to do so as the last operation before tying off, after the body and the wings (if any), and to bind them onto the shank with the butts towards the eye and the tips over the bend of the hook; they are then wound forward in close turns over their own butts and finally whip-finished behind the eye. The novice, and often the more experienced, tend either to leave insufficient room for the hackles between the eye and the body or to misjudge what room there is; either way they reach a point of having to finish up right against the eye, which usually manages to get itself mixed up in the whip finish : the result is at best a badly balanced fly—" all head and no shoulder "—and good balance can only be achieved if the hackles are centred almost one third of the distance from the eye to the bend; further the security of the finishing of a fly tied off in such circumstances might be suspect. We are indebted to Richard Walker for suggesting a far more satisfactory method, one which

I now use exclusively on every type of hackled fly I dress: instead of leaving the hackles until last, I tie them in as soon as I start to dress the fly, tying in their butts as soon as I have made sufficient turns of the silk, starting from near the eye, to secure it; I tie in the hackles with their butts *towards the bend,* so that their tips are lying across the eye, where they remain until the rest of the fly is completed and are then tied in in the usual way. By this method the space to be devoted to the hackles is determined before any other dressing is done, the shank around which they are to be turned is uncluttered except for the preparatory bed of silk, and the butts, which will be additionally secured by the dressing of the body are also usefully employed in the bulking, where necessary, and the shaping of the body. If it is intended that the hackles shall be mixed, with their fibres intermingling, they can be tied in together and subsequently wound together: however if they are to be kept separate, as, for instance shoulder and head hackle, they are best tied in separately, with sufficient turns of silk between them for the rear one to be wound upon.

The foregoing, of course, refers to conventionally placed hackles: when the fly is to be reverse-hackled—with the hackles at the bend-end of the shank—they are still tied in first, after the shank has been close-whipped from eye to bend, but with their butts pointing forward toward the eye and their tips to the rear; however they should be wound and secured as the immediately subsequent operation, before a start is made on the body.

Hackles on a conventional dry fly should be tied in face up, so that when wound their natural concavity inclines the fibres forward: this helps them to resist the forces of air and water which, in casting, will tend to pull the fibres backward into a "wet fly" attitude and prevent the fly from sitting properly on the water. Since most wet fly hackles *need* to incline backward rather than forward or upright they are best tied in face downward. The above applies to hackles tied in initially in the way I have described earlier, with their butts to the rear: if the "text book" method is used, with the butts tied in pointing towards the eye, then the reverse applies; dry fly hackles should be tied in face-down, and wet face-up. Reverse-dressed dry hackles, whose butts *must* be tied in pointing forward, should be face-up so that the wound fibres incline towards the bend (which is the head-end of such flies).

TYING SILK

I have referred up until now, and for the sake of clarity shall continue to do so, to tying " silk ", although personally I rarely use it: instead I dress most of my flies, and all my dry flies, with stocking-darning nylon; this is obtainable at negligible cost from any haberdashery department, mainly in various shades from fawn through olive to dark brown and also colourless, and primary colours can also be got with a little extra trouble if they are required. The virtues of this nylon thread over conventional tying silk are many: it is a fraction of the thickness but many times as strong; so strong is it that if you attempt to over-tighten you are in more danger of cutting your finger than of snapping the thread —the great bugbear of the novice. It will be seen that the pessimist can make many extra turns without substantially increasing the bulk of his fly, while the confident dresser, who will not make those extra turns, must finish up with a far more delicate fly, and one which is necessarily lighter. Waxing is unnecessary with nylon thread, though it *can* be waxed the more readily to accept a dubbing, although possibly a faint smear of varnish is better for this purpose. There are of course some dressings which require proper tying silk as an integral part of their make-up, mainly because of its colour properties—I have in mind the yellow body of the Greenwell's Glory and the purple base of the Imperial—but in these cases the required bit of silk can be tied in as part of the body material. Finally it is not essential to varnish the head of a nylon-tied fly, provided it is properly whip-finished, for I have rarely experienced one coming undone.

For nymphs and many wet flies I frequently use neither tying silk nor nylon, but do the whole dressing with copper wire. One of the main requirements of these flies is that they shall sink, smartly and without fuss, and thereafter reject any encouragement to return to the surface. To facilitate this, lead or wire is incorporated in the dressing of many patterns, so why not dress the whole fly with wire? This was demonstrated effectively in the case of Sawyer's Pheasant Tail Nymph, publicised by the late Oliver Kite, which incidentally although designed for the chalk streams is a successful Border pattern. The wire which I employ mainly is secondary armature winding obtained from odd items of scrap electrical equipment; this has a rich treacle-toffee colour imparted by a corrosion-resisting treatment which is lacking on ordinary bright copper wire. The wire I use varies from gauge 42 S.W.G., which is four thousandths of an inch or equivalent in diameter to nylon of one and a half pounds breaking strain, to gauge 33 S.W.G. (ten thou' or about 6 lb. b.s. nylon) depending on the size of the fly I am dressing: thus for a number 14 hook I use 37 S.W.G., which is .0068". If this seems unduly pedantic I apologise, but I feel that the only way to be consistent in fly dressing is to understand the materials I am using; every time I dress a standard Polo Nymph on a size 14 hook I use five inches of 37 gauge wire, so ensuring that all these nymphs are carrying the same weight and will not be irregular in performance. For practical purposes wire should not be so fine that it snaps easily but should yet be fine enough to bed down neatly on the hook. Wire should be used in substantially the same way as silk, except that great care should be taken to ensure that it is not allowed to twist; this means that it should be employed in short lengths, each turn being passed from hand to hand, and not wound on off a spool since this would put on a twist with each turn : twisting quickly results in kinking, and fine wire will easily break where it is kinked. My method with a nymph is to bind the wire in close turns from near the eye to the bend, where I tie in the body materials and the tail if there is to be one; I then work back to the thorax which I build up to whatever bulk of wire I need and thereafter complete the fly in the conventional way; if there is to be a hackle this will have been tied in at the beginning. A whip-finish in fine wire is put on in the same way as with silk; a wide loop should be maintained to absorb the twists which will accrue with each turn, and for this reason also it is best to limit it to three turns until you are sure that you can manage more.

Many professional dressers prefer to use lead rather than wire for the weighting of nymphs, primarily I suspect because it is quicker—the number of careful turns needed with wire *is*, frankly, time-consuming; because of its greater density also, a lead weighting must necessarily be less bulky than one of wire of equivalent weight. Lead, of course, cannot be used in *lieu* of tying silk, and must itself be secured firmly with the silk. The most common form in which lead is used for fly dressing is as a (relatively) fine wire, which is wound on in a few close turns under the thorax and then overwound with the silk: it can, however also be obtained in sheet form (usually for photographic purposes at about .003"—almost a foil). This can be cut into thin strips and wound on in overlapping turns or else cut to a steeple-shaped taper: the base of this narrow triangle is secured to the shank by oblique turns of the silk over the bottom corners, and then the remainder is wound over itself to form a compact rounded mass. This latter method is possibly the neatest of all, but as with copper wire it requires rather more fiddling.

BODY MATERIALS

Broadly speaking, any material which will allow itself to be wound round the shank of a hook can be regarded as a potential fly body dressing: apart from traditional things like furs and feathers, and less traditional stuff such as raffia and elastic, we have at our disposal a whole range of man-made fibres and plastics including Lurex and nylon line; indeed in the field of reservoir fishing there are " flies " which owe far more to the chemist than to nature. A reactionary by inclination, I have a personal preference for artificial flies which are made from traditional and natural materials; in point of fact I have yet to hear of a man-made material which can compete with nature in the dressing of a dry fly: the exception is Lurex, which is infinitely superior to metallic tinsel where it is required, but then tinsel is not a natural material anyway. Lurex is tougher and much lighter than tinsel and cannot tarnish, and it can easily be cut with scissors into narrow strips if bought in sheets: however I find it best if purchased, very reasonably, in spools. Possibly among nymphs a better case can be made out for *ersatz* materials; closely wound nylon makes a translucent and life-like abdomen though I doubt if it can compete in the fishes' affection with stripped peacock quill: however synthetic raffia, especially when dressed over silver Lurex, when wet simulates a succulent translucency which is undoubtedly sufficient to fool a fish.

Among traditional body materials there are only two of an exotic nature, apart from seals' fur, of which I make regular use: these are the ubiquitous peacock herl and also condor herl, natural and dyed. Peacock herl needs little enlargement from me since, with pheasant tail, it is one of the first materials to which the novice fly dresser is introduced: there are a couple of tips though, neither particularly original, which a beginner may find useful. First with unstripped herl: two or three strips may be tied in at the bend, or in smaller flies perhaps one strip, doubled at the middle; instead of winding on the herl by itself, twist the strands clockwise round the tying silk about the same number of times as it is anticipated that there will be turns on the fly, and then wind on the herl and the silk together. The idea of the preliminary twists is that they will cancel out those which will be put into the herl as it is wound onto the shank, and the reason for combining the silk with the herl is that the latter is a very delicate material and the silk will absorb tension (which might otherwise be sufficiently excessive to snap the herl) and at the same time will overlay the herl stems at some points, so strengthening the dressing. Because of the delicacy of peacock herl and its vulnerability to fishes teeth, it is wise whenever possible to rib it with fine wire, unless the dressing calls for a silk ribbing as in the case of the Abergavenny or the John Storey.

When it is required to strip peacock herl in order to use the quill only, the best way of going quietly mad is to try and do it with a sharp knife or razor blade as is too often recommended: it is much easier to use an ordinary soft india rubber, and gently to *erase* the fibres. When quills are intended for the abdomens of nymphs there is no need to be too fussy about stripping them cleanly: most free-swimming natural nymphs have bodies fringed with fine tracheal gills, and a few fibres left on the quill serve admirably to represent these. A strand from any part of a peacock's tail feather can be used for stripping to a quill, but the ones which carry the pronounced pale stripe which gives the realistic segmented effect to a fly's body come from the " eye " itself: since the eye strands are of little value for herling they are therefore best reserved for quills: they are slightly more difficult to strip than the plain bronze, and also inclined to be more delicate.

Peacock quills are easily broken and become even more so as a result of the dehydrating effect of age, when they also tend to split when wound on small hooks: this can be mitigated by keeping the prepared quills steeped in a thin vegetable or animal oil, such as olive or neatsfoot, and this also enhances their translucency; if anyone should feel that the presence of an oil might affect the sinking properties of a nymph, then glycerine is also quite effective. Personally I use neatsfoot oil for all types, and keep a quantity of prepared and steeped quills in an envelope made of greaseproof paper.

Condor herl is one of my weaknesses. A dedicated conservationist at heart, paradoxically I live in fear that the Peruvian authorities will clamp down so completely on the export of this magnificent bird's feathers as to deprive me of my supplies! Condor herl must be one of the strongest things in nature weight-for-size, and to my mind is perhaps the best of all body materials for a dry fly, yet strangely has been largely overlooked by most fly designers. It is strong enough to resist continual punishment from both ham-fisted fly dressers and fishes' teeth, yet at the same time produces a fly body of amazing realism and apparent translucency, not only to the human beholder but also quite evidently to the fish. For the idle fly dresser, such as myself, it can be used as a substitute (often more effective than the original) for almost any other material: I have used it with success on a Grey Duster (variant) in natural and a Dogsbody (variant) dyed fawn; on variants of the Rough Olive (dyed olive), Borderer (dyed blue-grey) and with deadly effect on a Black Gnat, to say nothing of a countless assortment of Sedges, for which it is ideal; my only regret is that it is too short on the flue to use as a substitute for peacock herl!

In default of condor, satisfactory body herls can be made from the pinion feathers of our larger native birds—swan, goose, turkey and of course heron: the not-quite-so-large also can be extremely useful on smaller flies; I use duck primaries frequently, while rooks and crows, especially carrion crows, provide excellent herls for small black-bodied flies. Bear in mind that the fibres of almost every feather (except the "working area" of cock hackles), and especially flight and tail feathers, have a web, and that web is a herl.

Another very useful, effective and virtually costless body material is clipped hackle; one might almost call it substitute condor herl: its use finds employment for many hackle feathers which would otherwise be thrown away on account of their being slightly oversize or of poor shape. Those which are too large are not of value for this function, since as I have explained earlier these will be too coarse in the stem and in the fibre interval, which for this purpose needs to be fairly dense. The feather should be clipped parallel to the centre stem and at a distance of about $\frac{1}{16}''$ on either side of it, depending on the size of the fly and the body-thickness required: this is most easily done from the tip towards the butt and not, as with preparing a feather for hackling, the other way about. If the initial trim produces too fat a body, further clipping can be done after the fly is dressed, and if a tapered body is wanted the feather can be clipped tapered or the fly trimmed on completion. Clipped hackle is not a material favoured by professional fly dressers because of the time needed for preparation.

HOOKS

If I were asked to describe my ideal hook, on which I would prefer to dress most of my flies, and all my dry flies, it would be as follows: " stainless steel fine wire, medium shank, round bend, forged but not reversed, wide gape, short point, tapered eye ". For reversed-hackle dry flies the eye must be turned-up, but for other types I do not think it is important whether the eye is turned up or down—though perhaps for wet flies and nymphs the latter is preferable from the point of view of appearance—or even straight. The specification I have given above may seem complicated, though something similar can be said in describing accurately any fish-hook, and other factors added. I have gone into this in much detail so that I can discuss and give my reasons for each characteristic in turn.

My choice of STAINLESS STEEL is not because of its non-corrosive properties but on account of its silvery appearance. I was privileged to be slightly—very slightly—involved in the birth pangs of John Goddard's book " Trout Fly Recognition "[1]; like many other great works this had its origins in an enthusiasm for something for its own sake—in this case the photographing of natural aquatic insects in or on their own element—the idea of publication came later. I was able to see many of his original photographs, in the form of transparencies, projected onto a screen, and was especially fascinated by those taken from beneath the water of flies resting on the surface, just as the fish would view them. There were of course, many more of these than could

---

[1] " Trout Fly Recognition "; John Goddard; A. & C. Black; London.

FLY HOOKS, GOOD AND BAD

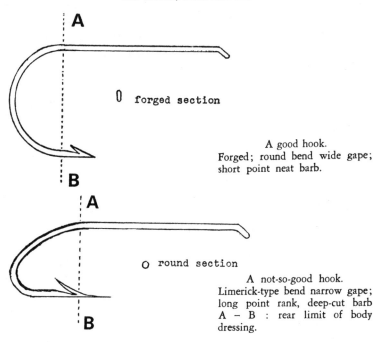

O forged section

A good hook.
Forged; round bend wide gape;
short point neat barb.

O round section

A not-so-good hook.
Limerick-type bend narrow gape;
long point rank, deep-cut barb
A – B : rear limit of body
dressing.

be included in the book, but all had one thing in common—the predominating impression of a burst of silver light: wherever a part of the insect impinged upon the water—feet, abdomen, tail, wing-tip—there was a splash of quicksilver; the colouring of the insect was secondary. In the interests of comparison John also photographed several artificial dry flies in the same way and the impression was the same; every hackle and tail-fibre pressing on the surface produced a spark of silver light; there was only one obvious difference: hanging down in the middle of it all was the black, ugly lower part of the hook. And that is why I use silvery hooks, especially on dry flies.

" MEDIUM SHANK ", I think, speaks for itself: the alternatives are " long " and " short ". Longshank hooks are best reserved for Mayflies on Border waters, while shortshank by their nature leave very little room for any but a rudimentary dressing, and because of the unbalance dry flies will rarely fall right.

I choose a ROUND BEND because to me it seems the ideal shape for a fly hook. The bend on a constant radius provides the strongest profile, gives the best shape for hooking and holding in this type of fishing and at the same time gives the greatest economy of outline. To explain what I mean by this we need to consider the shapes of other bends such as the limerick and its relatives: assuming that for our purpose the shanks of hooks are parallel to their points, on a roundbend hook the barb will be found to be approximately opposite the back end of the dressing, so that the point and barb are neatly and inconspicuously tucked in under the fly and within the area of the dressing. Most other bends cause the point and barb to be set back, sometimes quite a distance behind the dressing, where they cannot help but be obtrusive. A roundbend hook also does not need to be extended so far between the completion of the bend and the barb as do the limerick-type patterns; it is necessary in the latter to give the hook room to get round the edge of a larger fish's mouth.

A FORGED hook is one whose wire has been flattened from side-to-side to provide it with an oblong section with rounded top and bottom, in contrast to unforged, or regular, whose section is left round. Forging, and the section it produces, makes for a hook of greater strength in the direction from which the main stress is to be anticipated, and in fact does for the wire a similar service to that which a round bend provides for the whole hook: the two in combination allow of the use of slightly finer wire— always to be sought after. A further benefit of forging lies in the fact that the oblong section makes for a firmer-tied dressing, since it has less opportunity to slip about than on a round section.

I have specified forged *but not reversed* because reversing so often goes hand-in-hand with forging: a reversed (or kirbed) hook is one whose bend has been offset—the whole bend, that is, not simply the point (that is known as " snecked "). I do not much like either on a fly hook. In buying forged hooks or flies dressed on them attention should be paid to the sizes : there exists a scale of forged-reversed hook sizes which many manufacturers follow and which differs from the standard " Redditch " scale because the offset point of these hooks provides a larger gape relative to the length of shank: a size 14 forged-reversed can be as large as a size 12 regular, but this scale is often still employed when the hook is merely forged and not reversed as well.

WIDE GAPE. The gape of a hook is the distance between the shank and the point, and within reason the wider the gape the greater the chance of securing and maintaining a firm hook-hold; I say " within reason " since clearly if the gape is too great it will unbalance the whole fly: it is inadvisable to be dogmatic, but were I asked for a rough guide I would say that I prefer a gape which is equal to about five-eighths of the shank length, which is the distance between the back of the eye and the commencement of the bend—the straight part on which the fly is dressed. A wide gape performs a similar service on a straight hook as the off-setting does for a reversed, except that it gives an equal chance of hooking well on either side. It might be argued that surely a wide gape on a medium shank must be similar to a narrower gape on on a short shank, sized up; however the Redditch scale, which is the one most people use these days, is related to the gauge of the wire, so that the latter hook would inevitably be coarser.

SHORTPOINT. The beginner is often attracted to longpoint hooks because they look so much more deadly; the long, tapering point seems so much sharper than a stubby one, but there are pitfalls. Firstly that long, tapering point is much more easily blunted or broken, and secondly if only a light hookhold is secured—if bone is encountered under a thin covering of skin—the longpoint may not be able to penetrate far enough to engage the barb. My own choice is for the shortest point obtainable (the length of point being the distance between the tip of the point and the tip of the barb), and I like to see a straight knife-edge from tip to barb; if this knife-edge is kept honed the point will have, and retain, far more penetration than any longpoint. Hand-in-hand with a neat shortpoint goes a neat barb: a rank barb has the same attractive appearance of, and similar drawbacks to, a long point: it looks deadly because of the fearsome way in which it sticks out, but the more it does stick out the greater resistance it offers to penetration. The barb is produced by slicing the wire of the hook, and a rank barb often means that the slice has gone deep, so that the point is likely to be broken off easily. Too rank a barb can lead to messy extraction from a well-hooked fish, and this can be distressing if the fish is not large enough to be kept.

A TAPERED EYE is one wherein the short length of wire which is to be formed into the eye is tapered before bending; if such an eye is examined it will be seen that the end of the wire, where it is butted into the beginning of the shank, is substantially thinner than the shank itself; this makes for a much neater eye than an untapered or ball-eye, and is to be found on all good fly hooks. If a hook or fly sounds too cheap the eye should be looked to, for therein may lie one of the reasons for its cheapness.

There was a convention, now largely ignored except by the very pure, that dry flies should be dressed on hooks with turned-up eyes and wet flies on turned-down. I have heard many specious arguments to justify this, one being that different types of knot should be used for dry and wet flies which result in the leader-points coming away from the eyes at differing angles; or the converse, which is that since a dry fly is on the surface and a wet fly is beneath it, it is necessary in the interest of naturalness to *make* the points come away at differing angles. Nowadays I think most sensible anglers use the same knot for both dry and wet flies (in my case it is the four-turn half-blood), and whether one uses up- or down-turned eyes is largely a matter of personal choice. A turned up eye *is* desirable for reversed-hackled flies, but of that more later.

Chapter Seven

ARTIFICIAL FLIES

(1) *The Reversed-hackle Dry Fly*

MY EARLIEST introduction to the reversed-hackle fly goes back many years to a day when I was weatherbound in my club's " fishing lodge ", which was a room among the outbuildings of our riparian landlord's house. Leafing through a pile of old sporting periodicals I happened upon an article by David Jacques in which he described a hackled Mayfly of his own devising: this had a raffia body and the main (olive) hackle at the bend, while there was a much smaller olive hackle just behind the eye. The effect was to keep the entire hook clear of the water, though he evidently still regarded the eye end as the head, since the tails—three strips of pheasant tail—were in the usual place. I was quick to copy the idea, and on my own waters in the following mayfly season it worked like a charm. Inevitably over the years my version has evolved: I have only ever put tails on my first effort; these soon broke off and the fly went on catching fish, so I forgot about them after that: with my conversion to condor herl this, in natural, soon replaced the raffia, and was found to be an improvement. I had begun to become aware of the attraction to my Border fish of a touch of bright orange, and had meanwhile noted the inclusion of orange hackle in a number of traditional Mayfly patterns: these two lines of thought gelled at about the same time that I became convinced of the efficacy of the multiple hackling on Border dry flies, and the result was inevitable: my Mayfly pattern now has large olive and orange hackles at the bend, small ones in the same colours at the eye, and natural condor herl in between. For all I know it may be useless on a chalk stream, but on my own waters it is supreme.

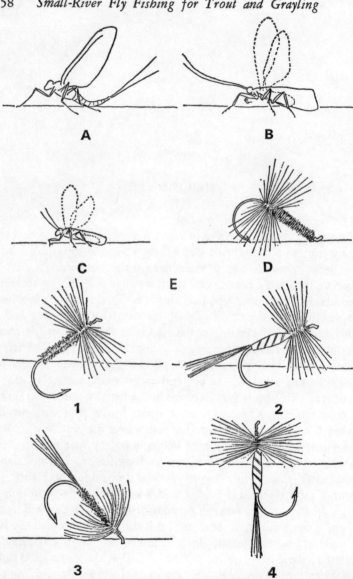

THE THEORY OF THE REVERSED HACKLE DRY FLY ON BORDER STREAMS

A: attitude of dun.
B: attitude of sedge.
C: attitude of small stonefly.
D: attitude of reversed hackle dry fly.

E: Some possible attitudes of conventional dry flies:
1: herl body, no tail.
2: with bushy tail.
3: poor quality hackle.
4: Silk body, sparse tail.

Curiously, or possibly because I am not very bright, it did not at first occur to me to adapt my success with the Mayfly to smaller dry flies—not until I became associated in friendship with Peter Flint of Presteigne. Upon Peter's shoulders had fallen the mantle of Cosmo Barrett or, to be correct, he had acquired the tackle and fly-dressing business of the latter after his death (in 1964), having already absorbed much of his near-supernatural fishing mystique as a result of years of angling together.

Cosmo Barrett, whose name is almost unknown outside the Welsh Border country, was one of the small band of fly dressers and designers to whom we are indebted for most of the Border flies which serve us so well today; as long as fly fishing is practised there he will be commemorated in his Barrett's Bane and Barrett's Professor (no connection with the sea trout and loch fly). Both these flies have reversed hackles, and at one time were very popular indeed in places far from their inventor's homeland—for many years he dressed them for Hardy's, who distributed them.

If I have not already made myself clear, a reversed-hackle dry fly is one which is dressed back-to-front, with the head end at the bend of the hook and the tail at the eye, only there are no tail whisks as such and there are no wings: the hackles are tied on just short of the bend so that the point and barb are among the hackle fibres. This has the effect of ensuring that, when the fly is fished completely dry, no part of the rear end of the hook can enter the water, and when it is fished awash the bend of the hook is largely hidden by the hackle. The eye end (and this is why I have emphasised a turned-up eye) sits naturally on the water in much the same way as a small portion of the abdomen of a natural insect, especially if the artificial is herl bodied, and the overall effect is much nearer to the attitude of a natural fly than is that of the conventional forward-hackled artificial. Theorists have from time to time dismissed this type of fly, mainly on the ground that the hackling round the hook masks the point and hinders its penetration, but I have found it to do nothing of the sort: indeed this very characteristic turns itself to the fisherman's advantage, though not in a way which its critics envisage—when the fly lodges among twigs and leaves it can often be retrieved by withdrawing it so gently that the hackles guard the hook against entanglement, whereas a conventional fly, no matter how delicate its treatment, must in similar circumstances inevitably get caught up.

I have mentioned earlier that the forces of air and water acting on a fly during casting have the effect of forcing the hackle fibres backward along the shank, which can cause a dry fly to sit awkwardly on the water, and that in conventional hackling an attempt can be made to combat this by arranging for the natural concavity of the hackle fibres to work in a forward direction. However with a reverse-hackled fly the opposite applies; the fibres are still forced backward, but in this case it is *forward* as far as the fly is concerned—into a more natural, rather than unnatural attitude. I have a strong suspicion that this factor, as much as any other, accounts for the efficacy of the reverse-hackled dry fly.

My earlier remark that no tails are necessary on these patterns may have seemed rather sweeping to anyone who has not used them, so perhaps I should elaborate. When I began tentatively to try reverse hackling on dry flies other than Barrett's Professor and Bane, I at first faithfully reproduced whatever tail dressing was specified, having the fibres sticking out over the eyes: this proved an irritating nuisance when it came to tying on the fly to the point, and after a time I decided to see what happened if I dispensed with the tails. The result was—nothing—even with the erstwhile bushy-tailed Abergavenny. The flies proved every bit as acceptable without as with their tails, and this confirmed in my own mind the previously growing suspicion that the only real purpose that whisks serve on a dry fly—spinners possibly excepted—is as an aid to buoyancy, which on a reverse-hackled fly is superfluous. After all there are large numbers of very killing dry flies which do not have whisks, but it is noticeable that for the most part they possess bodies formed of buoyant materials. All this of course does not apply to tags, most of which have been designed into flies with a purpose and retained because they have, presumably, fulfilled that purpose: the Orange Tag springs to mind, and it is no more difficult to dress in the tag on a reversed fly than on a conventional; it can be formed into a collar with loose ends, which can be made to lie over or under, or on either side of the eye, without seriously interrupting the tying-on of the fly.

I am not going to suggest that a reverse-hackled fly is superior to an ordinary one in all circumstances, although my own experience on my own waters is that it is mainly so. This superiority is most marked on streamier and broken water, and I have noted that there is more parity between the two types as the water smooths down until on very quiet stretches the conventional pattern will sometimes serve better; why this should be I cannot even conjecture. Nowadays I dress all my Border dry flies, apart from Barrett's Professor and Bane, both ways, but with heavy emphasis in favour of the reversed hackle.

(2) *Border patterns*

It is not my intention here to provide a catalogue of fly dressings: many of the patterns I have mentioned are well known and adequately described elsewhere—notably in Courtney Williams' Dictionary,[1] so I propose to content myself by enlarging on the less well-known Border patterns and variants, some of which enjoy a local success in inverse proportion to their obscurity. Most of the artificial flies I am going to discuss are dry ones, though nearly all can be used semi-sunk or wet (though not the latter if the fly is reverse-hackled) if circumstances so require, in which case the substitution of hen hackles for cock may be worthy of consideration.

DOGSBODY. Had I not already mentioned that this fly was my sheet-anchor I imagine that the fact must by now be apparent to the percipient reader. To perpetuate an already overworked *cliché,* if I were under the necessity of becoming a one-fly fisherman, this is the fly I must inevitably choose. For this reason I make a conscientious effort to keep it in reserve, and not to tie it on until artificials more appropriate to the fly on the water have been tried and found wanting.

The Dogsbody under its present name and incorporating this particular body material was originated by Harry Powell, a barber of Usk, in about the year 1924; however in general appearance the prototype must be older than that, since he was himself at the time trying to simulate a pattern provided for him by a client. His dressing is as follows:

Body: Brown tying silk dubbed with camel-coloured dog's hair, ribbed with flat oval gold.

Hackle: Red cock in front, grizzle (barred black-and-white from a Plymouth Rock) behind.

Whisks: Three strands from a cock pheasant's tail.

[1] " A Dictionary of Trout Flies "; A. Courtney Williams; A. & C. Black, London.

Mr. Powell gives as hook sizes Nos. 14 and 16, and I find these fair enough—14 for trout and 16 for grayling. However I have also found that with trout, if I am not getting the anticipated reaction to my 14, instead of going down to 16—which is the usually successful expedient—I fare much better by going up to 12, even on thin water: yet another imponderable!

Over the years my own versions of the Dogsbody have evolved, though never very far from Harry Powell's original. I have dispensed with the strands of cock pheasant from the tail since these have a habit of breaking off early in the life of the fly, and substituted a bunch of red hackle fibres—not just the usual five or six, but at least a dozen. In spite of my plentiful domestic supply of camel-coloured dog's hair I have experimented with fawn condor herl, and found it to be at least as effective, and also obviating the need for ribbing; clipped hackle has proved equally useful. In hackling I have been unable to improve much on Mr. Powell's specification, although I have found that badger serves as well as grizzle, than which it is perhaps a little easier, and certainly cheaper, to obtain in quality; somewhere along the line I tried turning the hackles round—putting the grizzle at the head, after the fashion of Barrett's Professor—and fancy that I detected a slight advantage. Predictably I have dressed it reversed, and that is the form in which I mostly use it nowadays.

Having reversed the hackling *and* the hackles, and substituted condor herl for dog's hair, I had arrived at a pattern which to myself I called the " Reversed Condor Dogsbody ", but it began to dawn on me that by now I *had* evolved too far from Harry Powell's design to justify the continued use of his name, even qualified by the addition of " Variant ", although in my own mind I was still using a Dogsbody and everything I have already said about it still applied. Friends insisted that here was a completely new pattern and that it should have its own name; " Welsh Terrier " was suggested and it has stuck.

WELSH TERRIER. I do not regard this as a substitute for the standard Dogsbody but as an improved alternative *on rougher water*: thus if the water tends to brawl I turn to the Welsh Terrier but where it smooths down again I turn back to Dogsbody. The dressing is:

Hook: 12—14, up-eye.
Body: Fawn condor herl.
Hackles: Reversed; head (nearest the bend) cream badger; shoulder: two red cock from different capes or at any rate of varying shades.

The reason for the attractiveness of the Dogsbody and the Welsh Terrier has yet to be satisfactorily explained; they look, let's face it, like nothing in nature and yet fish will accept them for almost anything in nature. Even when they are preoccupied with good hatches of fly but are disinclined to look at the official representations, they will very often come to one or the other, and they seem always to be especially effective when there are clouds of black gnat over the water. Courtney Williams, while confirming this attractiveness, suggests that the Dogsbody is less than a sheet-anchor since there are times, he says, when the fish will have nothing of it: my own experience is that the only occasions on which it has failed, have been after everything else has failed too.

I must emphasise that this is only my own experience; I am not proffering these flies as the universal ultimate killers—no such thing can exist, thank Heaven. It is entirely possible that the flies will be less effective on another's line, whereas one which kills consistently well for him might fail for me. The success of the Dogsbody and the Welsh Terrier in my hands may be more than partly due to my complete confidence in them, built up over many years; who knows that, had the Dogsbody not worked well for me the first time I used it (whenever that was) by now my confidence might well have attached itself to quite a different pattern?

BARRETT'S PROFESSOR. Once one has reverse-dressed a Dogsbody it is not difficult to see why the Professor is so successful; they look very much alike and had the Professor been designed by Harry Powell it might well have come down to posterity as the " Sheepsbody ". The hackling is very similar as is the body out-line effect, and the difference in the body-colours is only a matter of shading, providing a useful variation on some occasions. Sheep's wool for body dressing enjoys a high popularity among home-dressed Border flies (which is no doubt echoed among Border fishermen since supplies of it can be obtained from almost any barbed wire fence). The dressing of Barrett's Professor is as follows:

Body: Natural sheep's wool, preferably of a fawny shade (usually found on the underparts) ribbed with fine gold wire.

Hackles: Reversed; head-hackle (nearest the bend), white or grey; shoulder-hackle (two if necessary) red.

Perhaps the real genius of Cosmo Barrett was in evolving two flies each of which is a foil to the other. Uncannily when one fails the other can usually be relied upon to succeed, and *vice versa*.

BARRETT'S BANE. This fly is a straightforward reverse hackling of the Hereford Alder, for which excellent pattern credit is generally accorded to the late Canon C. F. Eagles of Coughton in Warwickshire, although his original version differs from the popular modern one. Barrett must have known the Hereford Alder well, but this need not dim the inspiration which resulted in his hackling it back-to-front. The dressing of both is as follows:

Hook: 12—16 (for grayling); Courtney Williams also advocated 10.

Body: Herl from the centre tail feather of a cock pheasant, ribbed, if required, with fine gold wire.

Hackle: Blue dun.

In his original dressing Canon Eagles had purple silk underlaying and showing through the pheasant tail, and this I can recommend—it is a device used with equal success on the Imperial, under heron herl. The Canon chose a browny-dun hackle in the first place but I don't think that this makes a difference on Border waters; it would need to be natural and very rare, and I find that dyed hackles are just as effective.

HEREFORD PHEASANT TAIL. I am not suggesting that the Pheasant Tail is an obscure pattern, indeed it is one of the most universal and it must be a rare fly box which does not have one or two in it: it is a successful all-round representation of any number of insects, wet and dry, but perhaps comes most into its own, more lightly hackled, as a spinner, and is a highly regarded Border fly. The dressing is:

Hook: 12—16.
Body: Herl from the centre tail feather of a cock pheasant, ribbed with fine gold wire.
Hackle and tail: Honey dun.

So much is well known, but I have included it here in order to place it in juxtaposition to the two previous patterns, Barrett's Bane and Hereford Alder. The bodies are the same, the hackles different. One day, preparing to dress both, or rather all three patterns, the idea came that since I proposed to use two hackles on each fly, a composite might be as effective as either, and I thereupon made a single fly with a pheasant tail body and one honey dun and one blue hackle. As far as I am concerned the composite proved to be better than either, both conventional and reversed, and now has a permanent billet in my box. The only problem was, what should the hybrid be called? I suppose that " Hereford Pheasant Tail " meets the bill as well as anything.

JOHN STOREY. This fly was originated by the river-keeper on the Yorkshire Rye whose name it bears, though it has been suggested that it is based on a much older traditional pattern known as the Orl Fly (vernacular for Alder) or simply the Peacock. It is regarded by some as infallible on its native river and enjoys a reputation as a killing pattern both for trout and grayling much further afield, not least on my own Border waters. Here it can be (I do not know why) very effective towards the end of mayfly time when the fish are getting choosey.

The modern dressing is:

Hook: 12—16.
Body: Bronze peacock herl (from the eye feather).
Wing: Small pale single whole breast-feather from a young adult mallard, dressed upright or slightly forward (teal or partridge are also used).
Hackle: Red or rusty-red cock.

Older dressings include a rib of bright crimson silk, and this, with the substitution of a suitable extra hackle in place of the wing, is the favoured variant on Border waters.

RED TAG, WORCESTERSHIRE GEM, ORANGE TAG, TREACLE PARKIN, WORCESTERSHIRE WONDER. These flies, or more correctly this fly —for believe it or not all these names refer to one pattern, with a choice of tags—started life as a highly successful wet grayling pattern, but nowadays are regarded as equally useful wet or dry, for grayling or trout. As far as I am able to deduce its history, the Red Tag originated on the Teme in the middle of the nineteenth century, and was then called the Worcestershire Gem: towards the end of the century it found its way to Yorkshire, where it was an immediate and lasting success, and it is presumably there that the variation to Orange Tag emerged and became known as the Treacle Parkin; sometime thereafter it was re-exported in the latter form to the county of its birth, where it is now popularly known as the Worcestershire Wonder. Once more it is difficult to understand what the fish see this fly as, although it does seem most effective when one or other of the small stoneflies are about— which on Border waters is most of the time—especially the willow fly in the autumn. The dressing is:

Hook: 12—16.
Body: Green peacock herl from the sword feather.
Hackle: Red cock.
Tag: Red or orange, wool or feather.

I have given the body material as green peacock herl, because that is correct: however many fly dressers appear to ignore this and use the common-or-garden bronze: since to my knowledge these flies catch plenty of fish—I cannot say whether more or less than with a green body—it is a choice perhaps best left to the individual. The tags were originally made from self-coloured exotic feathers such as ibis and Indian crow and later from substitute materials, usually dyed swan; nowadays however the preference seems to be for tags of bright orange or red wool, sometimes fluorescent.

ABERGAVENNY. The pedigree of this rough-water dry fly might well be given as " by John Storey out of Dogsbody ". It first showed its qualities on the River Usk near the town whose name it bears, but I can vouch for its effectiveness on most lively Border streams; the rougher the water the more it seems to like it and it has the advantage of being fairly easy to see in such circumstances. Dressing:

Hook: 10—14.
Body: Bronze peacock herl ribbed with bright crimson silk.
Hackles: Red cock in front (two if necessary), badger behind.
Tail: A considerable bunch—18 strands at least—of red saddle-hackle fibres.

BLUE VARIANT. We are indebted for this fly to Mr. E. C. Coombs, late of Tenbury Wells (to whom credit must also go for the most generally used pattern of Hackled March Brown). I have never been clear what it was intended as a variant of, since it is quite different from both the Blue Quill and the Blue Upright (both of which are good Border flies). Be this as it may the Blue Variant has few equals on Border streams when small and medium olives are hatching, and has the additional virtue of being also very effective when small stoneflies are on the water. The dressing is:

Hook: 14—16.
Body: Rabbit's blue underfur ribbed with pale yellow silk.
Hackle and whisks: Olive.

ROUGH OLIVE. This is another well known pattern, Halford, Skues and Bridgett all having a hand in its evolution. My reason for including it in my list of "underpriviledgeds" is to draw attention to a variant body dressing (not my idea) which I think improves and simplifies it. The dressings are as follows:

	Skues	Bridgett
Hook:	14	14.
Body:	Brown-olive heron herl, ribbed fine gold wire.	Medium-olive swan herl, ribbed fine gold wire.
Hackle and tail:	Hen, dirty-brown, dark at centre, yellowing toward the tips.	Olive hen.

Both these patterns are winged, Bridgett's being snipe, rolled and advanced, and Skues' conventionally of dark starling, but for Border work the substitution of an extra hackle is to be preferred, mixed with or behind the olive, of darkish blue dun cock. The variation I am suggesting is the substitution on the body of brown-olive condor or clipped hackle; this is altogether more robust and also more buoyant, without detracting in any way from the fly's appeal. The concensus in favour of hen hackle is interesting, especially since this is primarily a dry fly, but it certainly works; nevertheless the inclusion of a stiff cock's hackle in the non-winged version would seem to be of all round benefit.

Intended primarily as a representaiton of the large dark olive (for which in springtime I would favour a No. 12 hook), the Rough Olive can be made to stand in satisfactorily for most of the up-winged flies by sizing down as far as 16 as the season advances and also by lightening the colour a little.

ORANGE OTTER. This has the reputation of being one of the most killing grayling dry flies in existence (especially in autumn when trout also will take it keenly), not only on Border waters but generally. It is fairly well known, and again my reason for including it here is to suggest the substitution of condor herl as the body material. When I give you the dressing you will see why:

Hook: Normally size 16—more rarely, and for trout, 14.
Body: " Pale biscuit-coloured underpart of an otter's throat, soaked overnight in picric acid solution, then boiled for a few minutes in the same solution to which has been added an equal volume each of red ink and water ". The body is divided into two equal parts by the hackle.
Hackle: Short red cock.
Tail : Red cock.

I find that for the body the employment of condor herl of a bright red-orange does not diminish the appeal of the fly, while at the same time it obviates the need for chemistry and also the demise of an unfortunate otter.

The Orange Otter was the creation of the Rev. Edward Powell, sometime rector of Munslow in Shropshire, a past master of Border fishing with a marvellous understanding of the tastes of Border fish: to him we are also indebted for such proven Border flies as the Baby Sun Fly, the Doctor, the Ermine Moth, a version of the Grannom, the Paragon—a sort of universal sedge—and the Split Willow. It is noticeable that of these flies no less than four employ rabbit's fur; also, like many of his contemporaries, he made extensive use of picric acid for producing yellow shades—again in four of the above patterns.

GRIZZLY DUN. In naming some of the men to whom we owe a debt of gratitude for outstanding service to Border fly dressing, one whom we must include is Walter M. Gallichan: among others he has left us with the Grizzly Dun:

Hook: 14—16.
Body: Yellow silk, waxed or oiled to olive, like a Greenwell.
Hackle and tail: Grey badger.

The Grizzly Dun is very useful when both small stoneflies and up-winged flies are about, as is another Gallichan fly whose name sums up what it is all about—the Borderer.

BORDERER. This little fly has a big reputation; it is quite unlike the Grizzly Dun yet kills well among the same range of insects: the two work together in much the same way as Barrett's Professor and Bane, with one taking up the running if the other falls by the wayside. Its dressing is:

Hook: 12—16
Body: Rabbit's blue underfur (rabbit again!) with a red silk tip.
Hackle and tail: Rusty dun.

The red silk tip of the Borderer leads me to another important Border pattern with the same characteristic.

IRON BLUE (HARRY POWELL). Among the several Iron Blue artificials which he mentions and the half-dozen-odd which he describes, Courtney Williams curiously does not include this one; and yet if you go into a tackle shop and ask for an Iron Blue, you are more likely than not to get a fly which bears a closer resemblance to Harry Powell's pattern than any other. I have hedged a little on this because I have very often seen shop " Iron Blues " offered on size 12 hooks, and while a 14 *might* be acceptable for the early variety I cannot really conceive of a true representation of an iron blue dressed on anything larger than a 16. The dressing is:

Body: Mole's fur dubbed onto crimson silk, of which a couple of extra turns are made behind the tail to form a small tip.
Hackle and tail: Iron blue dun.

In addition to the red tips (which when treated with an oil-based flotant will assume a purple-brown colour) there is a superficial similarity between the Borderer and Powell's Iron Blue which *could* account for the existence of the latter dressed on larger hooks; perhaps it should be regarded as a " Borderer Variant "!

STOKESAY. This is a Border fly which stands on its own merit, but which I am especially happy to include as a tribute to its inventor, the late Mr. C. V. Hancock, for many years angling correspondent of the *Birmingham Post*. He dressed it originally as a substitution job for an odd, unnamed fly which had disintegrated under an onslaught of fish, and found that it continued the good work, especially at mayfly time; its name derives from the stretch of the River Onny which he was fishing at the time of the fly's first success.

> *Hook* : 12—14.
> *Body* : Darkest claret clipped-hackle, ribbed with fine gold wire.
> *Hackle* : Rusty red cock.
> *Tail* : Three strands from a cock pheasant's tail.

RED HACKLE. I suppose that this must be regarded as the basic trout fly, the direct ancestor of half the artificials in the world and of such Border flies as Coch-y-bonddhu, Coachman, John Storey, Abergavenny and Red and Orange Tag. Courtney Williams traces its ancestry (somewhat tenuously, I feel) back through Cotten, Walton and Dame Juliana Berners to the Macedonians no less. The fact that it is less used than some of its progeny is possibly because of its sheer simplicity and lack of sophistication. The modern dressing is :

> *Hook* : 12—14.
> *Body* : Bronze peacock herl.
> *Hackles* : Red cock.

Sometimes a tail is included of three fibres from a cock pheasant's tail. It is quite deadly on my waters, especially when dressed reversed with two hackles of slightly differing shades of red.

WELSH FUSILIER. I have mentioned this fly as the best medicine on my own waters when black-tipped soldier beetles, or other similar species, are in profusion in the waterside meadows, but it is actually well worth putting on any time during the summer when fish are disinclined to take notice of anything else; possibly its gaudy colouring shocks them into aggression! Military men, and especially Welsh military men, will recognise the aptness of its name, for the black collar flash of the Royal Welsh Fusiliers might well have included them in the description of " black tipped soldiers ".

Hook: 12 (up-eyed if reversed).
Body: Hot-orange clipped hackle.
Hackles: Three cock hackles: 1 (head), hot orange; 2, furnace; 3, darkish slate-blue.

DADDY LONG LEGS. I promised earlier in this book to give the dressing of my own version of the crane fly, and this would seem to be an appropriate juncture. The hook should be as for Mayfly, size about 10 or 12; it is unwise to be dogmatic about size, since the daddys themselves come in assorted sizes, according to species. Next take six pairs of cock pheasant tail fibres and put a simple overhand knot in approximately the centre of each pair: these are to be the legs; single fibres *can* be used for this purpose, but I have found them to break rather easily in use. These legs are now tied in by their butts onto the hook shank, starting at a point about a quarter of its length from the eye: they will, of course, be in pairs on opposite sides of the shank; the front pair should incline sharply forward, the second forward of square and the third slightly toward the rear: exact positioning can be adjusted with extra turns of silk. Next tie in a longish-fibred olive or brown-olive hackle behind the legs, and after it is wound it should be divided by " figure-of-eighting " so that most of the fibres stick out on either side rather than above and below. Lastly the whole of the uncovered parts of the hook shank (including the bit between the front legs and the eye) should be close-wound with condor herl of a dirty olive or browny-grey colour, and this should also be worked between the legs in order not only to improve appearance but also to lend stability to the set of the legs, which will incline to drag backward as a result of casting.

Condor herl for this purpose, and indeed in all circumstances where close herling is the only requirement, is best taken from near the tip of the feather where the individual quills are fairly fine: strips taken from nearer the butt of the feather are much coarser in the quill (and also much stronger) but give a ribbed appearance which, though ideal when this effect is required, do not lend themselves so well when a close-pile effect is wanted.

NYMPHS

Compared with the long list of wet and dry flies, the number of named and effective nymph patterns suitable for Border fishing is quite small; a high proportion of these are cut-down versions of traditional wet and dry flies, and some of the more satisfactory of these are the nymphs of the Greenwell, Tup's, Hare's Ear and Pheasant Tail (not to be confused with Sawyer's Pheasant Tail Nymph, which is even more effective). In recent years has come the realisation that the really successful Border nymph needs to be purpose-designed and not merely adapted, and that its requirements are firstly a slim and translucent-seeming abdomen and secondly a bulky but lifelike thorax in which is incorporated a certain amount of weight. These two latter factors fortunately go hand-in-hand, since much of the bulk of the thorax can be provided by winding on lead or copper wire, while the technique of doubling and re-doubling feather strips such as pheasant tail over the back of the thorax provides a lifelike representation of incipient wing-cases; hackles are normally regarded as superfluous. Many such nymphs, similar in fundamentals but differing in detail, are being plied with success about Border streams at this moment with hardly a name between them—often even to the men who make and use them. I know of one, however, which is outstanding.

POLO NYMPH. This highly regarded Border nymph was the creation of Peter Flint of Presteigne, and like one or two other successful patterns came into existence as the result of a happy inspiration. Deciding to go fishing at short notice and finding himself without any nymph patterns he sat down hurriedly to knock some up quickly: at a loss for a suitable handy material for the thorax he pulled a tuft of wool from an old polo-necked sweater which was hanging alongside his bench and tied it in, and so the Polo Nymph was born. Although I do not believe that the material for the thorax is more important than that which he used for the abdomen, I still wish that I could quote the make and number of the wool from which that old sweater was knitted; alas, I fear that we shall never know—it was, as I have said, already old, and no one has any recollection from where the wool came originally. Nevertheless I have thought it worthwhile to take a close look at a piece of the original wool, and find it extremely interesting: most vari-coloured knitting wools obtain their effect as a result of being made up of a number of different coloured twisted strands, or else by having their strands vary in colour as they go along, so that the colour of one half-inch of wool may be different from the next. In the case of Peter Flint's sweater, the wool was made up of an assortment of different coloured *fibres* which must have been dyed separately and brought together in specific proportions before the wool was spun, so that the reason for its attractiveness becomes obvious. A careful count of the fibres from pieces of the wool emerges as follows: bright green, 30 per cent; dark brown, 30 per cent; bright red, 25 per cent; daffodil yellow, 15 per cent. Knowing these colours and their proportions it is a comparatively simple matter to synthesise the mixture from a similar assortment of self-coloured wools, or, possibly better, seals' furs. However the colours and their proportions need hardly be taken to be arbitrary—since their use in the first instance was fortuitous—and it might be possible by experimentation to arrive at an even more attractive mixture.

I have already mentioned the importance I attach to the material used for the abdomen of this nymph, and this is a slightly orangey-yellow silk stout-floss, which when wet appears to change in colour and consistency to a rich, translucent mahogany, and I am sure that this effect can be enhanced by providing an underbody of silver Lurex. It is ribbed with fine light-brown or fawn tying silk, though if copper wire is used for weighting it can also be employed for ribbing. Peter Flint's own dressing for his Polo nymph is as follows:

Hook: Size 14, leaded under thorax.
Tail and wing-cases: 6 or 8 strands from the centre tail feather
of a cock pheasant.

Abdomen: Pearsall's silk stout-floss, shade 156, ribbed with fawn tying silk, slim.
Thorax: Wool, colour-mixture as above, rather plump.

QUILL POLO NYMPH. This is a nymph pattern whose effectiveness is such that it would be a disservice to my readers were I to fail to include it: it has not been named previously so that the name, which seems accurately to describe it, is my suggestion.

Hook: Size 14, weighted.
Tail and wing-cases: 4 strands of cock pheasant centre tail, doubled and re-doubled for the wing-cases.
Abdomen: Stripped peacock quill over silver Lurex underbody, the turns of the former only just touching so that a glimmer of silver can be seen to sparkle between them from some angles.
Thorax: Seals' fur, colour in similar proportions to those given for the Polo Nymph above but with the addition of a little black, and very thoroughly mixed.

BROWN SQUIRREL NYMPH. Similar in outline and general appearance to the last two patterns, but using different materials, the Brown Squirrel has been an outstandingly successful nymph with me personally. Visually there can be no better way of imitating the tails of a swimming nymph than by using the tips of pheasant tail fibres, but their chief disadvantage is that they can get broken off very early in the life of the fly: the Brown Squirrel uses the brown/black/fawn hair from the tail of a Canadian pine squirrel instead, and also for the wing covers, while the same animal provides the body fur for the thorax.

Hook: Size 14, weighted.
Tail and wing-cases: About 12 strands from the tail of a Canadian pine squirrel, doubled and re-doubled for the wing-cases and pinched off at the tail to leave about ¼″ projecting and if possible showing a little of the black at the base.
Abdomen: Bronze coloured nylon raffia ("Raffene") over silver Lurex underbody, counter-ribbed with fine gold wire or nylon tying thread.
Thorax: Dubbed with well-mixed fur from the back of a Canadian pine squirrel.

Nylon raffia when opened out is about $\frac{7}{8}''$ across, so that it is best split lengthways into three or four strips for use on this nymph body; however it becomes somewhat tender when wet (as well as realistically translucent), hence the ribbing.

Since, as I have pointed out, the Polo Nymph, Quill Polo and Brown Squirrel are similar in outline and general appearance, it is possible to permutate the various materials in several ways: this in fact I do, particularly in respect of the hair for tails and wing-cases which I now normally use on all patterns.

AMOROUS SHRIMP. This is my own dressing for use in early summer when the shrimps change to their " mating livery " of bright orange. It can be fished either as an upstream nymph or as an across-and-down wet fly.

    Hook : Size 16 double, weighted.
    Body : Bright amber-orange wool or silk (a useful fluorescent
             variety is known as " arc chrome ").
    Hackle : Bright ginger cock, dressed palmer-fashion, and
             counter-ribbed with fawn tying silk.

My reason for choosing a double hook is two-fold: first it is essential that this pattern is fished along, or at any rate close to, the bottom, and in fast water a double supplies much of the extra weight needed: second, my grayling, the re-opening of whose season often coincides with the height of the shrimp mating period, can reject a larger single hook so fast that unless one can actually see them move to the fly it is usually too late to do anything: a small double can't be got rid of quite so easily.

UPSTREAM WET FLIES

It is important to understand the difference between conventional —that is to say down-and-across—wet flies, wet flies which are fished upstream like sunk dry flies, and wet flies which are fished upstream like nymphs. Ordinary downstream wet flies are easily recognisable; they are soft-hackled (with hen if poultry hackles are used) with the hackles dressed to incline backwards; if winged, the wings are dressed to lie back over the body, and are tied in over the hackle, which is often a throat hackle only. This style of dressing (which is common also in lake flies) has evolved to give the fly the best " entry " and enable it to fish in the most lifelike way *in the fishing style for which it is designed,* that is, down-and-across: it is not intended for use upstream. It does, however, in some forms lend itself to being fished upstream as an *inert* offering, in the film or just below it, to represent a hatching insect (the Invicta is supposed to imitate a sedge) or else a drowned one —freshly drowned insects are buoyant. For this purpose many dry flies are themselves just as suitable, if left untreated with flotant or well spat upon: many anglers find success by beginning with an unoiled floating fly and allowing it to get more and more waterlogged until the ideal condition for the fish is revealed. Wet flies made specifically for this purpose are usually dressed in very much the same way as dry flies, but with soft hackles.

Wet flies for fishing upstream like nymphs—with movement—with the exception of those such as the Hare's Ear which look like nymphs anyway, are mostly dressed as " spiders ": that is to say that they are lightly (two turns) hackled with longish, soft, webby, mobile feathers such as partridge breast, snipe's rump or wing (not the pinions, of course), starling or jackdaw throat; these are dressed squarely to the shank or even inclined slightly forward, and not towards the rear as is the case with a downstream fly, and this has the effect of giving them the appearance of life when they are moved in the water: most have slim bodies and no tail. Well-known patterns which are successful on Border streams are the Black Spider, Black-and-Peacock Spider, Snipe and Purple, Snipe and Yellow, Partridge and Silver (the spider version of the Silver March Brown), Partridge and Orange and Partidge and Yellow Spiders. With the yellow- and orange-bodied flies mentioned above (as with many other wet flies) a distinction must be made between body materials which are affected by soaking in water and those which are not; for example, orange silk when wet will acquire a translucent mahogany appearance, whereas cotton or synthetic fibre can be expected to remain orange; which kind one uses will depend on the effect required. Spider patterns can also be used downstream of course, though usually still benefit from imparted movement: for upstream work at least I prefer mine weighted, and for this I normally use fine copper wire wound evenly along the whole shank.

Chapter Eight

GRAYLING

MUCH OF what I know about the grayling has already come to
light at various points in this book. I treat it on at least an equal
footing to the trout, but if only because elsewhere the scales are
heavily weighted against it I feel that I can best demonstrate my
respect for it by according it a small chapter on its own.

Most chalk stream fishers regard grayling as vermin (a heart-
ening exception was the late Major Oliver Kite), perhaps with
justice if on their waters the grayling show signs of getting out-
of-hand and swamping the trout, at the same time offering poor
sport. Some Border anglers share the same view, too often because
they have accepted mindlessly some hand-me-down dictum that
grayling are bad for a river in the same way as otters and herons;
the fact that otters prefer eels and herons most relish frogs and
that both are necessary to the health of a fishery, and that Border
grayling give at least as much sport as trout, are truisms which some
people nevertheless have difficulty in accepting.

Other Border trout fishermen, perhaps the majority, never give
the grayling a thought and may even be unaware that they are
present until they encounter the rare occasion when one fortuit-
ously attaches itself to their line: for whatever they may do elsewhere, Border grayling rarely succumb to conventional dry fly
methods, and usually need to be looked for in different places and
at different depths than those in which trout are to be anticipated.
It is quite possible for an expert trout fisherman, fishing with only
trout in mind, never to realise that there are grayling in the water.

The grayling has my personal respect because frankly I find it
more difficult to catch than trout—harder to tempt and harder to
hook when tempted: weight-for-weight it gives at least as good

sport as trout and—more important to the man who has to travel
a distance to his fishing and has to take his sport as he finds it—
seems always more ready to have a go; whereas trout will go down
and do nothing for long periods between feeding, grayling are on
the lookout most of the time. Border grayling once hooked are a
considerable handful, especially if they get downstream of you in
the swift water and use their big dorsal fin like a kite in the
current. They lack the resourcefulness of trout though, which
causes the latter to head unerringly for a tangle of roots or weed,
nor do they seem able to emulate the trout in that infuriating con-
juring trick whereby it manages to transfer a hook on a tight line
from its mouth to a convenient underwater root or reedstem, leaving a foolish-looking angler putting pressure on an inanimate
object!

I consider grayling one of the most beautiful of all fish, and
every time I catch one I am captivated anew by the delicate
iridescence of its colouring which, regrettably, fades so quickly
after death: I regard them as better eating than trout, as do many
of my acquaintance, although this must always be a matter of personal taste. Its scientific name, *Thymalus thymalus,* is supposed to
derive from the fact that it smells of thyme, though I have never
been able to come to terms with this; I have wondered whether
perhaps the legend may have derived from the name instead of
vice-versa. Personally I find the smell of freshly caught grayling
more reminiscent of cucumber than anything else.

Unlike the trout, the grayling is of course a shoal fish, though
perhaps on my own waters " group " would be a better adjective,
since a large shoal is something of a rarity, except perhaps in
winter. I do not often find more than three or four grayling together, and then they are usually of a size; surprisingly I do not
frequently come across small grayling—that is less than two years
old and shorter than ten inches—although obviously they must be
there and in considerable numbers; at three years old and about
three-quarters of a pound they are more likely to be found in pairs,
and after that they tend to become solitary.

Except for big old fish, grayling do not have holts to which to
repair to rest or when alarmed as do trout, but congregate in the
depths of their pool. The holt of the solitary old fish will always
be deep also, usually beneath the overhang of the roots of a tree
which has made a scour. It is sometimes possible, on quite a small

stream, to look down through four or five feet of water in such a place and see a massive grayling swim out momentarily and seize something in the current: it is quite a different matter to try and catch him with a fly, though.

A hen grayling produces about two-and-a-half times as many eggs as a trout, though much smaller and, because of the more open method of spawning, more vulnerable to predation. This could nevertheless be one of the reasons why grayling too easily become a problem on some waters, especially highly fertile ones to which they have been introduced.

Grayling like to lie on the bottom and are rarely to be found in mid-water and even less frequently near the surface except when in shallow water; I think that there may be some atavistic instinct which causes them to minimise the possibility of attack from underneath: I *have* encountered them browsing just under the film but only when attractive food is in profusion on the surface, and then in fairly slack water. They are not really built for sur-face feeding, their comparatively small mouth lies below and behind their rather pointed snout, and is actually perfectly adapted to bottom feeding. This alone makes it surprising that they are prepared to rise so freely, but what is even more remark-able is the delicacy with which they can rise on occasion: the general impression of a grayling rise is of a somewhat boisterous and splashy one, but large grayling are quite capable of dimpling so quietly—especially in the evening in placid reaches—that one is left wondering if one is looking at rises at all, but perhaps at the dipping patterns of tiny insects.

Unless actively feeding on a gravelly bottom grayling will usually lie around the deepest part of the deepest pool, which is one reason why their presence is not often suspected. If their im-mediate inclination is for surface food they will travel swiftly to the surface and back for each insect, but if their taste is for nymphs and the like they will look for them while cruising slowly along the lower shoulders of their pool, occasionally flashing up and down again to take a likely one in mid-water. Contrary to commonly held beliefs, insofar as the grayling is allegedly a fish of arctic origins and therefore a creature of fast cold water, they actually tend to seek slower water than do trout and are not noticeably so fond of colder water—indeed they are not found much north of the Highland Line. Grayling have a narrower temperature-comfort range altogether than trout, since they also dislike the water too warm; I have found the latter still to rise happily in water temperatures up to 62°F, given good oxygenation, but grayling will pack up well before that. They appear to be constitutionally the more delicate of the two species—they are notoriously bad travellers, and much easier to kill (the 1969 epidemic of UDN almost wiped out our grayling, though the trout population was not seriously depleted)—and demand a far greater purity of water than trout and indeed than any other freshwater fish: if one has grayling one can at least be sure that one has very clean water.

In general grayling like smaller mouthfuls than trout, particularly in surface food: I have not known Border grayling go much for mayfly although these occur at a time when the grayling, spawning completed, should be looking for substantial food to speed recovery. Nor do they seem to fancy very dry flies, and if they come to them at all they either come short or miss them altogether, and this may also be something to do with the problem of eyesight which we discussed earlier. I have found that the best chance is with a small fly fished almost drowned, or even an upstream wet fly on a greased leader.

Grayling on my waters are perhaps easiest to catch on an across-and-down wet fly, particularly during the trout close-season when the water is usually higher and more coloured and a sinking line can be used; one reason for this is that one is in firmer contact with the fly and the fish are more likely to hook themselves: however one cannot really regard this as one of the higher forms of the art although it can be great fun.

My favourite way of fishing for grayling (perhaps because I find it most successful) is when one can be found visibly feeding in shallow water: they can be doing this in two different ways. In one of these the fish will have found itself a fixed feeding position in a narrow area of quiet surrounded by streamier water; a favourite place is just over the down-stream edge of the tail of a pool, so that the fish often appears to be lying in the fast water at the top of a stickle, although its movement will show that it is having little difficulty in maintaining station. From this position it will be seen to be making deft movements to either side and upward to intercept nymphs and other underwater morsels and more rarely surface flies. To catch such a fish is quite easy given reasonable accuracy: a nymph cast from as near square as possible and pitched about a foot upstream so that it will come down past him not much more than an inch or so on his near side will usually do the trick; you need to tighten as soon as the fish, having moved to the nymph is seen to move away again: if you wait for the leader to move you will be too late. The other situation is when a good grayling is found to be what I call " browsing "; this is when, usually on a broad gravelly bottom under shallow but fairly streamy water, he is methodically pushing stones about and grabbing the nymphs and shrimps which are thus unceremoniously disturbed. A grayling doing this will shift surprisingly large stones and it could well account for their being provided with such well-padded snouts. The progress of such a fish is marked by small puffs of disturbed silt—" smoke signals " I call them—and these are often the give-away, for they will usually be seen before the eye can locate the fish itself. A nymph is again the answer, and a heavy one at that, even in shallow water, for it must pass him at no higher than eye-level for he will not be looking at anything above it. In this situation it is usually possible to cast from a more downstream position and again accuracy is fairly essential—not much more than a couple of inches to the near side —for he will be too preoccupied to notice anything further away. Tightening must again be by sight.

The dry or semi-dry fly I find more of an enigma, though whether or not this is peculiar to Border waters I do not know. I have already said that a half-sunk or drowned fly works better than a fully dry one, but even these have their problems when it comes to tightening. It is fairly well known that a trout will usually come only once to a dry fly, even if he isn't touched, and that he is unlikely to come again until either he has been rested or the fly changed: a grayling, however, will come again and again and again, provided he isn't pricked. Many of these rises are out-and-out misses—and can be seen happening to natural flies—and can be variously explained by eye-sight, the placing of the mouth, and the distance through which the fish has to rise, all of which have been discussed elsewhere in this book. When one tightens to a grayling rise, therefore, one usually does not know whether one is tightening to a hit or a miss, except on the rare occasions when one is close enough to see the action clearly: it is therefore extremely difficult to be sure if one's timing is right. There are many days on which fish are found to need less or more time in tightening—why I do not know—and with trout it is relatively easy to find out which: you miss the first one, have a fair idea why, and make the appropriate allowance for the next, and except on the odd particularly bloody-minded day you can usually get it right after not more than two or three have been missed. With grayling, however, the additional factor of the missed rise can make it very difficult indeed to come to terms with your tightening: you can get rise after rise and treat them all differently, and still not know at the end if you have been too quick, too slow, or just right if only the fly had been taken. I wish that I were in a position to give more conclusive advice about this, but I cannot even now consider myself qualified so to do: this is annoying, really, because there are people whom I know to have less trouble than I with grayling rising, but their action is instinctive and they are unable to say what governs it. One thing is certain, and that is that it is unwise to adhere to the trout-fishing dictum of waiting for the fish to turn down before tightening, because a Border grayling can reject a fly as he is turning.

There is a method of " fly fishing " for grayling which seems to have originated from the mists of time in my own Border country and which can be very effective: this is by means of the artificial " grasshopper ", although any resemblance to a natural grasshopper, colour apart, needs a resourceful imagination. A large hook is used—a 10 or 12 or perhaps a 14 double—and on this is dressed a considerable quantity of lead, tapered towards each end with the main girth rather forward, like a bomb: over this goes the dressing, and I have come across a number of versions for this, whose common denominator is that it should be green; silk or wool, dark green ribbed with light green (or *vice versa*) or else a rib of green peacock herl from the sword feather; older versions call for two strips of straw tied in at the head to lie along either side of the body, although natural raffia is more durable. The method of fishing it is to pitch it into the head of the run (" cast " is perhaps too refined a word), give it time to sink and then work it back sink-and-draw, or at any rate agitatedly. Normally the grasshopper is only really effective when fished through a really deep pool, for which it was no doubt orginally evolved, and indeed with many grayling holes, whose depth relative to length is such as to preclude any conventional nymph from sinking more than a short distance before it has passed over, it represents the only hope of getting a lure down anywhere near the fish: plenty of loose line needs to accompany the grasshopper onto the water to allow it to sink fast before drag sets in, but this must quickly be brought under control as soon as fishing depth is achieved. Many will look askance at the ethics of this method of fishing, but I feel that its use is justified if it is confined to the removal of big old grayling who can never be caught by purer means and whose intake of food could be better employed. It doesn't *always* work, anyway.

Chapter Nine

WATER IMPROVEMENT

THAT A stretch of fishing can be improved by good management is almost too obvious to mention, but in the case of the vast majority of Border streams there is virtually no management at all, and this is too often the result of circumstances than of lack of inclination on the part of many anglers. Management of any sort presupposes the expenditure of time and money, but most Border fisheries are held on short leases, or no lease at all, by the individuals or clubs who fish them. The riparian owner is usually a working farmer who reiterates frequently " I don't know nothin' about fishin' "—the implication being that he cares even less provided he can get the best price from the town-bred idiots who want to come and paddle in his stream. And indeed if you want to find a fool in the country you need to take him with you.

It follows then that anyone whose tenure of water is thus precarious is naturally reluctant to embark on the costly improvement of someone else's property when the result could easily be the loss of it at a better price brought about by its enhanced value. Individuals and clubs who have the good fortune to acquire the freehold of their own waters are very differently placed, as to a lesser degree are those able to negotiate a rare long lease. Riparian farmers who are alive to the possibility that a valuable asset can be further profitably improved are for the moment few and far between, though increasing, but where they exist they are short on knowledge of what is needed (not being anglers), and their " improvements " usually extend no further than the cutting down of every tree in sight.

In discussing water improvement, therefore, to be practical we have mainly to look at short-term and temporary expedients, against a background of what *can* be done given the time and the money.

By "water improvement" we mean the improvement of the fishing, both in the environmental pleasure of the angler as well as the quality and quantity of the fish he hopes to catch. I cannot think that many really *prefer* to do their fishing by crawling through brambles or to confine their casting to a series of flicks—any more than they prefer to catch small fish rather than larger ones—so that what we need to seek to do is to improve the amenities of both protagonists without allowing one adversely to affect the other.

Few Border streams (I except some hard-fished association water subject to heavy cropping) require restocking: natural regeneration is usually ample—I know of some streams where it is too generous for the good of the water—and stocking may only result in a head of lean undernourished fish. A given water will only support a given weight of healthy fish; add to their number and all will have less to eat; crop them sensibly and the result will be fewer but better fish; set out to improve their natural supply of food, and the result will be more and better fish. Our Terms of Reference, therefore, in the context of water improvement, are to increase the amount of nourishment available to the fish and at the same time enhance the pleasure of the angler both in his sport and in his pursuance of it.

The fish (if you exclude the angler who catches him) is at one end of a food chain which starts at the other end with alga and the minute animals which feed upon it; then come the larger animals such as nymphs and shrimps which eat the tiny ones and often the algae as well, until they themselves (and in the case of nymphs their adults also) fall prey to the fish; the higher the quality of this chain in all its links the higher will be the quality of its end product.

To improve the quality of the fish, not only is it necessary to improve the quality of the fishes food, but to *maintain that improvement*. Let me therefore say at once that to attempt "instant improvement" of the food supply by stocking the water with quantities of insect larvae and eggs, or shrimps or snails and the like, is likely to be about as profitable as putting the cash needed for them straight into the river; just as the water will only support a given weight of fish, so it will only support a given level and

variety of food creatures. Almost certainly a nucleus at least of all
the animals likely to thrive in a water is already there; adding to
their number without improving *their* food supply will only result
in underfed insects whose numbers will soon return to their
original economic level. Like the pounds which look after themselves if we attend to the pennies, what is required is that we
attend to the well-being of the food supply creatures, and that of
the fish will come about without further help from us, in this
direction anyway.

WEED

In seeking to improve the food supply of the fish, we must not
only improve his *habitat* but also the *micro-habitats* of the creatures
on which he feeds, but at the same time we must do our best to
reduce as far as possible his dependence on bottom food. The
answer to most of this is alga, moss and weed: alga and moss can
normally be left to look after themselves provided other circumstances are right, but a great deal of help can be given to weed,
which is the micro-habitat of vast numbers of underwater
creatures, many of them the free-swimming nymphs and larvae of
surface hatching insects. Weed, however, is at a premium on most
Border fisheries, but there are ways of encouraging it and of persuading it further to propagate itself.

By " weed " I mean underwater weed, not surface or emergent
plants which, while useful in moderation in giving cover to fish
and insects alike, do not have the food-harbouring propensity of
a dense sub-aqueous growth to offset their nuisance value if over
abundant; Border fisheries do not have an excess of these either,
anyway.

The principal weed on Border streams is the river crowfoot,
Ranunculus fluitans; it is one of the best for our purpose, which
is fortunate, since it is the only one which we usually have in quantity. Not long ago I came across a small bed of Ranunculus, and
because something about its appearance suggested that it might be
a slightly different species from *R. fluitans* (I subsequently found
that I was in error) I pulled up a handful, shook it well, and took
it home in a plastic bag for positive identification; having got it
home I stuck it in a jam jar filled with tap water to give it time to
flower so that I could count the petals and examine the stamens:

after it had stood for a week on a sunny window-sill I chanced to notice movement among the packed weed, and when I took a lens to it I discovered that it was alive with small life; there were literally thousands of tiny larvae and pupae, of many different species, squirming about in the water or grazing upon the algae which covered the stems—enough food animals to keep a fair-sized fish happy for days.

Other types of water weed *are* to be found, but rarely in a sufficient concentration to make them significant; where they are found they should be encouraged, for I doubt if there is such a thing as a bad weed in the context of fish-food harbouring: river crowfoot is our standby because it is the plant best adapted to the spate conditions which are a feature of Border rivers, and when a river luxuriates in other, less spate-proof weeds, its status as a Border water must be in question.

Although river crowfoot is an underwater weed and has no surface leaves, it emerges for the purpose of flowering—the daisy-like mass over the open shallows are familiar to most anglers. It has three main requirements—plenty of sunlight, a brisk flow of clean water and shallows of stable gravel. Small gravel is of little value since its shifting nature precludes a good root-hold, and most established Ranunculus beds will be found to be based on stones of the size of this book and upward: it will root in other places of course, such as clay or clay and small gravel, but is more likely to get washed away annually. The governing factor— as with the encouragement of all life, not least on Border streams —is sunlight; you won't often find a weed-bed in the shade. I remember well a shady stony shallow, of little fishing value because of its depth, across which it was necessary to carry an electricity line; the first thing the engineers did was to have all vegetation removed for fifty yards on either side, and we were furious; nevertheless by next season that stretch was a mass of crowfoot, and the fishing downstream of it improved dramatically: two of the factors were there already, and the moment the third—sunlight —was added, the weed-bed sprang to life.

There may be some streams devoid of Ranunculus simply because none has found its way there, or at any rate to their higher reaches (propagation is normally downstream), or it is possible for a severe winter to kill off an entire stock. If a place in a stream looks as though it should support the weed it is always worthwhile obtaining some and planting it at the top of the stretch chosen, making sure that its roots are well enough anchored to withstand a good spate. If it is river crowfoot you want, make certain that that is what you get; there are many different species of Ranunculus, each adapted to a special environment, so that it is always advisable to get your roots from a place in the same watershed which appears to be similar to the one which you want to colonise. Once a bed of crowfoot is established on a stretch of water it can be used as a nursery from which to try and establish it experimentally in other places, though if the bed is near the head of the stretch it can usually be relied upon to find for itself all the suitable downstream sites for colonisation.

Where what appears to be a weed bed is found in the shade— under trees, for example—it is likely to be not a weed but a moss known as *Fontinalis*; darkish green with " leaves " which give it a superficial resemblance to Canadian pond weed, it will probably be found to be living parasitically on the roots of a tree like a sort of underwater mistletoe; quite common on Border streams, it is a useful harbourer of fish food, and should never be discouraged.

However, even if conditions allowed it, we can hardly put down the whole of our stretch to weed; it would drastically restrict our fishing room and the fish, in any case, have other important requirements.

THE STREAM BED

Left to its own devices a river will always seek to make for itself the widest and shallowest bed; before the advent of modern man with his bridgeworks, efficient land drainage and intensive agriculture our rivers, apart from those in rocky gorges, were no doubt much broader and shallower than they are today, and for the most part bordered by marshes which allowed this. A broad shallow bed allows the water of a stream to follow a leisurely line of least resistance, and winter spates will tend to increase this characteristic unless they are constrained by obstacles such as trees or boulders or man-made impediments. Thus a river running over a gravelly substrata within a soft top-strata would, if untrammelled by obstacles, spread itself to wide ankle-depth and unhurried flow along its whole course. Such conditions are inimical to good trout and grayling, and where they obtain steps should be taken to counter and reverse them. In trying to make a stream fit for our fish to live in we must seek to concentrate the flow so as to give the greatest possible depth, a brisker flow and the incidental bonus of better oxygenation.

The secret of river bed improvement is to make the river do the work; to decide in advance what needs doing; to make the necessary dispositions while the stream is in quiet summer flow, and then to wait until the winter spates unleash their full power. Even when you are watching it happen it is difficult to visualise the fantastic force which quite a small stream can develop when in spate; only when the flood subsides does any realisation come with the sight of hundreds of tons of gravel shifted effortlessly overnight: I can think of one example where by clever manipulation a Border brook was persuaded to shift its bed *over thirty yards* to one side in the course of one winter.

While moving a stream about is not really an activity to be envisaged by an individual or a club which does not own the land in which it flows, it is worthwhile examining the methods by which it can be achieved because they are the same as those which, to a modified degree will be used to encourage concentration of water and increased depth and flow.

" CROYS "

The basic tool for the manipulation of a stream is the groyne or " croy ", which in its simplest form is a breakwater projecting into the current which will deflect the stream outward towards the other bank. The skill lies in the placing and the dimensions of the croy relative to the individual stream and the work which it is required to do; these cannot be laid down arbitrarily and can only really be determined by trial and error and learning by experience, but it is possible to lay down general guide-lines.

The best croy is made from stones bound together by sand, gravel and cement (all but the last can usually be found in the river bed): if it is to be located on a stone or gravel bed which at low level is clear of the water, it can be fashioned like a low wall, but if, as is more often the case, it has to be placed in the water, then the aggregate should be put dry into hessian sacks and these built into a wall. A less permanent groyne (and this is to be preferred by the man who lacks experience and is not sure of the

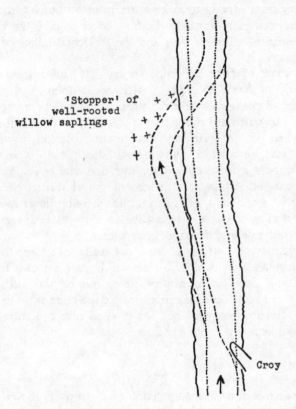

Original main course of current: $\longrightarrow$
Induced main course of current: $\longrightarrow$

USING A CROY TO CREATE A DEEP-WATER BEND

ultimate effect) can be made of wooden planks or sheets of iron held firmly in place by deep driven stakes on both sides, and buttressed to its full height by substantial stones on the down-steam side; lengths of tree trunk or concrete blocks can be similarly used. The placing of a croy is fairly critical both as to its position in its own bank and its angling; the latter is generally not less than 45° downstream of square to the current, but this can be effected by extraneous factors such as the contour of the river bed at that point and whether the site is on an existing straight section

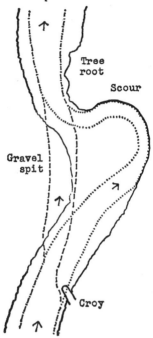

Original main course of current: →..........

Induced main course of current: →_ _ _ _ _

Using a croy to stop a scour which is threatening to by-pass an established tree, the effect of which would be either to create a divided current or else bring down the tree

or on a bend; however anything much squarer than 45° will at best be less effective and at worst result in the loss of the most solid croy, due to the sheer weight of water and undercutting.

The actual location of the croy will depend on what it is required to do; if its purpose is to scour the far bank with a view to making or increasing a bend, then its siting and aiming must be calculated again with reference to the shape and consistency of the river bed and also bearing in mind that the deflection will be rather less acute than the angle of the croy. A croy can be used to advantage to *stop* the scouring of a bank; in this case it will be placed upstream of the scour on the same side and its angle into the stream only sufficient to deflect the current from the scour.

In siting a croy great care should be taken that its inside end is butted firmly into the bank, so that the water is not able to circumvent it; if a bank is soft at the point of a croy's junction with it, some form of cladding, such as an iron sheet, should be placed to protect it until the new current-pattern has established itself. In general a croy should not be longer than the equivalent of one quarter of the width of the stream bed, and should taper down gently from the bank end to the outside edge, at which point its height should be about six inches above the water at normal summer level; this will mean of course that the whole croy will be submerged long before conditions of actual spate are achieved, but any attempt bodily to divert a heavy current can only end in disaster. This specification should not be regarded as arbitrary, but rather as a preliminary guide.

The sheer crude power of a river in spate must never be lost sight of, and before anything is done to tinker with the bed of the stream provision should be made to ensure that it does not get out of hand: prior to unleashing the current against a soft bank it should be decided how far it is required to go and what is to be done to prevent it from going any further. If there are no natural obstacles such as established trees, these must be created, and to do so means planning several years ahead, and this is of course something outside the scope of casual water improvement. The best way to establish a stopper to your deflected current is to hammer into the field at the chosen point several rows of willow stakes, each about a yard apart; over about three years these will establish themselves into well rooted trees, and it will be these roots which will bar the stream from further progress in that direction: as soon as the willows have established themselves they can be partly cut through near ground level and broken over to lie prostrate; every twig that is in contact with the ground will itself send down roots to reinforce the main ones, and the whole small grove will become a dense thicket of valuable fly cover; at the same time a useful windbreak will have been created, not normally affecting casting since it will eventually be sited round the rim of a scour. Should further initial control be necessary, the options will be: (one) a counter-croy above the scour; (two) a camp shedding of iron sheeting on the face of the scour; (three) the depositing of thorn bushes and the like in the front of the scour to break up the current: or all three. I must re-emphasise that the elemental force of a stream in flood should never be underestimated, and it is so easy to do so working in the deceptively tranquil conditions of summer level.

The kind of spate which is the most valuable (and also the most destructive) is the near " banker " when the flood is just contained within the existing banks of the stream : once it goes " over the top " and into the adjoining fields all its pressures are equalised and it makes no significant impression on the actual river bed.

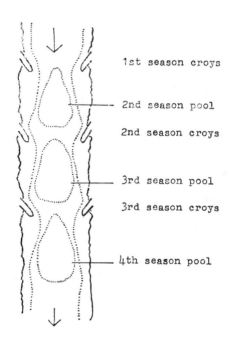

Water Improvement

DEEPENING

In order to concentrate and deepen the flow of a stream the same ideas apply as have been discussed above for moving its bed, which itself has the effect of providing a deep narrow channel under the scour. The difference is that instead of the siting of one croy on one side only to deflect the current, two (rather shorter) croys are placed opposite each other: these have the effect of each countering the other's deflection so that the current is concentrated

midway between them, and its force will very quickly excavate a
deep pool immediately below, banking the gravel on either side.
A long straight stickle, harbouring only small fish, can in this way
be made to provide a series of useful pools: you start by placing
a pair of opposed croys at the head, and leave them until next
season to determine the extent of the pool they will have exca-
vated; the next pair of croys will lie just below the tail of this
pool, and so on. It is often not necessary to provide a pair of croys
for this purpose, but to achieve it by opposing one croy to an
existing natural obstacle, such as a projecting tree stump or out-
crop of rock. The deepening of stretches of shallows in this way
is a comparatively simple matter, certainly not involving any minor
civil engineering such as is needed for moving the bed: since the
water is shallow at the outset all that is needed in the way of
groynes are a pair of stout planks, though it is important that they
should be very firmly staked—with deep-driven iron bars if
possible—and fully supported by rocks on the downstream side.

WEIRS

Whenever water improvement is discussed, sooner or later the
provision of weirs is mentioned, together with all manner of in-
genious suggestions for their simple construction. Apart from their
being looked on with disfavour by most River Authorities I do
not myself see any value attaching to a weir: it is true that the
water downstream of it is likely to be improved and better oxy-
genated, but what about *upstream* of it? Even a small weir will
cause a stream to back up to a surprising extent and form a " canal
stretch " which will probably become silted but which will certainly become the home eventually of any coarse fish which may be
about and also of a small number of cannibal trout. Neither is the
siting of a weir at the top of a stretch of water seriously to be
considered, since the reaction of one's upstream neighbour is not
likely to be favourable.

VEGETATION

Lastly we have to consider riverside vegetation, both the substantial sort in the form of trees and bushes and also the annual types
such as nettles and all the other plants which luxuriate by the

waterside in summer: several conflicting requirements need to be reconciled, and I believe that success in this reconciliation, perhaps more than any other factor, will determine ultimately the success of a fishery. Let us first look at the main demands of the interested parties.

Firstly water weed, which provides food and lodging for much of the early part of the fish's food chain as well as shelter for the fish themselves: this needs as much sunlight as it can get, and therefore the minimum of shade. Second, the adult flies, between hatching and returning to the water to reproduce and/or die: they need plenty of cover from predators, rain and wind—especially wind, which can keep them off the water, except by accident, for days if not altogether. (This applies equally to non-aquatic insects of interest to the fisherman.) For most flies the best cover needs to be dense and not too far from the water.

Thirdly the fish; they like cover, sometimes they like more cover than is probably good for their well-being, but they can manage without it in excess provided that there is reasonable shade for them to go to in conditions of bright sun. Shade is more important to trout than to grayling, for the latter can always lie in the depths if the surface light is too bright for them and still make quick trips to the surface for food: however in bright sunshine it is unusual to find good trout feeding anywhere but in the shade, which is one of the reasons why on open water in high summer rising is so often confined to early morning and evening in spite of good daytime incidence of fly; indeed in summer, when a day shows signs of being cloudlessly sunny and hot, in considering my *venue* for that particular day's fishing I will invariably opt for the stretch which offers the most shade: moreover I will take into account those stretches which I know to be well shaded for some distance upstream, for in that way I shall come in for cooler water also.

Finally the fisherman; he wants room to cast and room to put his fly on the water, given tolerable accuracy, without getting it hung up too often: he needs to be able to move along his water in reasonable comfort without resort to athletic exercise appropriate to an obstacle course, and without scratching and stinging himself to excess. At the same time he needs cover from wind for himself but also for his tackle, and he needs cover also to help conceal him from the fish.

From the outset it is necessary to make a firm distinction between bankside cover, whether annual or semi-permanent, which
does not to an appreciable degree overhang or shade the water,
and that which does, the latter normally taking the form of trees
or large bushes: let us deal with non-shading cover first. As I
have tried to emphasise, bankside cover for the harbouring of insects is as vital to the well-being of potential fish food as is aquatic
weed itself: to be ideal from all points of view it is best kept
low and dense, and one of its best forms for the assistance of
aquatic insects is young willow growth propagated as I described
earlier—that is cut and bent to a prostrate position and allowed
to grow thickly near ground level; naturally this should always
be done only in situations where it cannot seriously interfere with
the back cast, but with this in mind young willow is a much more
amiable proposition than are alder and hawthorn (the commonest
Border waterside trees) either of whose intractability with a
caught-up fly needs no testimonial from me; both hawthorn and
alder are somewhat slow growers and are also slow to root;
neither lends itself to propagation by layering. Hazel thickets
also provide good fly cover and windbreak, as indeed do most
deciduous trees and bushes.

Among annual waterside plants quite the most important is the
common stinging nettle; I have already made mention of its aphis
population, but it also gives harbourage to virtually every aquatic
and waterside insect—perhaps some instinct advises them of its
protective properties! Here, however, we have a ready-made area
of potential conflict: no one likes nettles, for a bed of them is
hardly a thing of beauty and to have to go and rescue a caught-up
fly from the middle of one can be quite unpleasant; good farmers
cut them or spray them, and with each nettle bed so destroyed is
lost a large slice of our insect population—and not only insects of
interest to the fisherman, for many species of butterflies and moths
live and breed in nettles. I am not going to suggest that an angler
bent on improving his fishing should go so far as actually cultivat-
ing nettles, but certainly those which he has he should leave be,
and content himself with making only a sufficient path through
them to allow him to pass unstung.

Shade vegetation, as opposed to that which gives fly cover and
protection from wind, can also be divided into two categories—
that which hangs low over the water, and overhead trees. Of the

former almost all is valuable in moderation, that is provided it does not cover relatively too great an area of water and provided it is possible without too much difficulty to get a fly beneath it: I am personally intolerant of branches which are allowed to droop so low that their lower leaves are actually in the water, rendering it impossible for even the most skilled caster to put a fly to the fish which are almost inevitably beneath. I have heard it advocated that " the fish should be allowed *some* sanctuary ", but have little patience with this philosophy; for one thing the fish have plenty of sanctuary in the form of lies made unapproachable by back-eddies and drag, to say nothing of their holts, and holes which are inaccessible to the fly by virtue of their great depth relative to their length; a trout whose lie is physically inviolate will eventually become a cannibal, and the whole stretch in his vicinity spoiled. In these days of rising rents and shrinking waters deliberately to leave water unfishable, which could with a few strokes of a saw or bill-hook—or even secateurs—be made fishable, is as silly as keeping money under the mattress instead of investing it safely.

I have just mentioned secateurs, and these are something which I almost always carry with me while fishing and would advise every angler of bushed waters to do the same: there is no better time than when fishing to recognise the places where one is not able to put one's fly and the twigs which most readily magnetise one's back cast, and to deal with them on the spot: continuous attention to them in this way can save a lot of sawing and chopping later, and a good pair of light secateurs can deal with most branches of up to almost an inch in thickness.

The main effect of larger trees, apart from harbouring insects, is to provide shade, and I hope that I have already demonstrated that while some shade is essential it is nevertheless a bad thing in excess; every stretch of fishing should have a balanced variety of conditions—of weed and open water, of fast and not-so-fast current, and of open sunny stretches alternating with shade. One cannot deal as arbitrarily with large woodland trees as with bushes and saplings, but if the former seem too numerous their effect can often be mitigated by being a little more severe on the latter. One situation which should always if possible be avoided is that where-in both banks of the stream are shaded, with the branches meeting overhead like the roof of a tunnel allowing little light to come from any direction; such places may contain the odd good fish but will make little contribution to the food supply of the water. I think that a fair enough rule would be that if one bank of a stream is shaded then the other side should not be, even if it means taking a power saw to a substantial tree; I don't think that it is too important which side of the river is opened up, although perhaps preference is best given to the side from which the sunlight will fall, not only from the point of view of the beneficial effect on the water but also bearing in mind the problems of the angler approaching the fish: the direction of the prevailing wind should also be taken into account.

From a fishing point of view one of the most difficult types of shade is that produced by a line of trees standing along one bank whose branches stretch right across and overshadow the water, the other bank being open; the spaces between the trunks of the trees are often filled with obscuring vegetation so that light is effectively excluded both from one side and overhead and is concentrated, to the fish's eye, in the strip along the open bank through which the angler will probably have to move in order to fish. The solution is unlikely to be that of wading up on the tree-lined side, since the roots of the trees will almost certainly have ensured that it is also the deep side, the food lane side and the side on which all the fish are lying. The only likely answer is to try and equalise the light, and if the removal of some of the trees is not possible then every scrap of smaller vegetation between them should be got rid of.

When any sort of cutting-out is to be undertaken I would emphasise that it should be cutting out and not rooting out; the latter is perhaps not something which will occur to the individual or small club, but some farmers and River Authority workmen (whose main concern after all is drainage), when faced with a fallen tree or one which looks likely to fall, will use their powerful equipment to drag out the whole thing, roots and all, rather than bother to saw it through above the still buried roots: once the roots have been ripped out the soil from which they were pulled will be more friable than that surrounding it, the current will move in and the result at best will be a widening and shallowing of the stream at that point: on the other hand should this point of weakness happen to be in the path of the set of the current a scour can be started whose ultimate limits would be anybody's guess; I have been witness to the loss of quite a lot of land to certain farmers as a result of this practice.

FLY BOARDS

Fly boards are normally associated with the chalk streams rather than with Border fisheries; their purpose is to offer egg-laying facilities to females of the Ephemeropteran genus *baëtis* secure from the depredations of such predators as the larvae of sedges, stoneflies and aquatic beetles. However several flies of this genus are of interest to us—small, medium and large olives, and iron blue—and have already been mentioned as having free-swimming nymphs, and adults which hatch from the surface film, and are therefore well worthy of encouragement. They have in common the fact that the females crawl down beneath the surface to attach their eggs to some underwater object such as a bridge-pile or a reed stem or the root of a tree, in which location they are often available to the bottom-crawling predator larvae mentioned above: if fly boards are provided many of them will avail themselves of them, and the result should be a general improvement in their population. Certainly it would be worthwhile to experiment with them on most Border fisheries.

A fly board is simply a thick plank, moored in the centre of the stream; it should be thick for two reasons: firstly because many flies will prefer to oviposit on the vertical surface of the sides rather than the underneath and secondly to lend it stability; both these factors may be better served by keel-weighting it—nailing some lumps of old iron to the bottom so that the top is almost awash, but without unbalancing it. The best place in a given stream for siting a fly board is probably best decided by experimentation; possibly the best type of position is in a pool of fair depth and even flow, so that the stability of the board is not prejudiced by waves and ripples: flies will shun an unstable platform. At least two mooring lines (one to each bank) are needed to hold the board steady, and these should be fixed to the upstream end of the plank, as far apart from each other as possible, again in the interest of stability. Needless to say the board should be so located as to make any contact impossible with the bed or sides of the stream, or with any object such as a submerged branch which could be used as a bridge by potential predators.

APPENDIX

Data kindly provided by J. B. F. Lloyd, Ph.D.

SINCE 1968 Dr. John Lloyd has been carrying out a detailed investigation into three fisheries held by the Gamefishers' Club in order to determine their productivity and potential. Members were asked to co-operate by providing the stomach contents and scale samples of fish killed, together with details of length and weight, date and time of capture, and other relevant information. Unfortunately (though no doubt predictably to those concerned with club administration) the response has not been so whole-hearted as one would wish, and in consequence the sample to date (some 73 fish) not really extensive enough to give this appendix the validity for which I had originally hoped. However the data is, I think, sufficient for my main purpose, which is to place the three differing waters in juxtaposition and so show how the differences affect the incidence of aquatic fauna and the consequent feeding inclination of the fish.

The first two Tables are concerned with the stomach contents of trout taken during the trout season. Since figures can be made to prove or disprove anything (his words were " susceptible to misinterpretation "), in passing them on, Dr. Lloyd has made certain emphatic reservations, which in my turn I pass on to the reader. These are, firstly, that the figures represent feeding efforts, and not actual food supplies: by this I mean that the units are individual animals, whether they were minute reed smuts or may-flies, and no account is taken of the relative differences in weight and bulk between various creatures.

Secondly that the data represent what was being eaten by catchable fish only, at the time they were caught, and not necessarily by all the fish in the stream: here " catchable fish " means those capable of being captured by conventional fly fishing, and rules out not only those lying in unfishable places but also those for the time being preoccupied with such foods as snails and possibly crustaceans, or grubbing in the bottom for creatures habitually living there. Thirdly some figures are known, for various reasons, to give a distorted picture of feeding habits, and these will be indicated and explained: however since the figures were expressed in percentages such a distortion in one animal unbalances all the others, and this unbalance must be allowed for.

For these reasons and because the overall sample is not so extensive as was hoped, we have deemed it best to express the results as " star ratings " in order to ensure that individual figures (which could well be subject to a tolerance of 10% either way) do not assume an apparent significance disproportionate to what may be their true value.

The streams concerned are all slightly alkaline: it would have been more satisfying to include an acid water in the survey in order to present a more balanced picture of Border waters generally, but we must take what we find.

Stream " A " is an essentially lowland water flowing through fertile farmlands and having a large gathering area: it is the most alkaline of the three (though this is of course a relative term—being alkaline does not make a river a chalk stream.) It has in fact a pH of 8.5 .

Stream " C " is only marginally hard and alkaline; it has a relatively small watershed in a hill farming area; the growth rate and average size of its fish are much smaller than in " A ", and its pH is 7.5.

Stream " B " is somewhere between " A " and " C ". Itself flowing in rich farmland, its water is nevertheless fresh off its extensive mountain gathering area; with a pH of 8.0 it is slightly hard and alkaline.

Table 1 relates to the presence of individual organisms found in the stomach contents of trout: that is to say if five mayflies and two stoneflies were found in one fish, each insect would nevertheless have a value of one.

Table 2 is concerned with the overall percentage of organisms in the whole sample for a particular river, and shows the proportion of individual members of a family or group of creatures eaten by all the fish sampled. Although the percentages upon which the respective ratings of the two tables are based are necessarily different, it is interesting to note the great similarity between the two sets of results.

TABLE 1

Surface insects, etc.		Stream "A"	Stream "B"	Stream "C"
Simulium (reed smuts)		***	***	***
Stoneflies		**	**	*
Caddis (sedge)		*	**	–
Ephemeropteran	Mayflies	***	*	*
duns & spinners	others	*	*	**
Terrestrial Flies (including spiders, caterpillars, etc.)		****	****	***
Sub-surface animals, etc.				
Simulium (reed smuts) larvae		*	*	**
Stonefly larvae		–	–	*
Caddis (sedge) larvae		*	***	**
Ephemeropteran	Mayflies	**	**	–
nymphs	others	*	**	***
Snails		**	–	–
Limpets		*	–	*
Shrimps		*	*	–
Aquatic beetles		–	–	*
Fish (mainly bullhead)		*	*	–
Grayling spawn		–	**	–

FOOD ORGANISMS REPRESENTED IN STOMACH CONTENTS OF TROUT

****	Organisms found in 60% of fish or over.
***	Organisms found in 20% of fish or over.
**	Organisms found in 10% of fish or over.
*	Organisms found in under 10% of fish.

TABLE 2

	Stream "A"	Stream "B"	Stream "C"
Surface insects, etc.			
Simulium (reed smuts)	**	***	**
Stoneflies	*	**	*
Caddis (sedge)	*	**	–
Ephemeropteran Mayflies	***	*	*
duns & spinners others	*	*	*
Terrestrial flies (including spiders, caterpillars, etc.)	****	***	***
Sub-surface animals, etc.			
Simulium (reeds smuts) larvae	*	*	*
Stonefly larvae	–	–	*
Caddis (sedge) larvae	*	**	*
Ephemeropteran Mayflies	*	*	–
nymphs others	*	**	***
Snails	*	–	–
Limpets	*	–	*
Shrimps	*	*	–
Aquatic beetles	–	–	*
Fish (mainly bullhead)	*	*	–
Grayling spawn	–	**	–

PERCENTAGE OF INDIVIDUAL ORGANISMS FOUND IN OVERALL SAMPLE

**** 50% or over of total.
*** 20% or over of total.
** 5% or over of total.
* Under 5% of total.

DISTORTIONS. The most immediately apparent of these is the very high rating for ephemeropteran nymphs on stream "C"; this came about as a result of concentrated and successful fishing by John Lloyd himself in April at a time of substantial hatches of spring olives, and his catches proved to be stuffed with nymphs: the rating indicates no more than that these insects occur on this water in fair numbers at that time. The second distorted figure is that of adult mayfly on stream "A", though this must be obvious since these are only around for three or four weeks of the season; stream " A " is the most easily accessible and *ipso facto* the most popular of the three, and is subject to a particularly heavy turn-out of rods at mayfly time: indeed I suspect this to be the only successful turn-out for some rods.

The low, but equally distorted ratings for molluscs and crusta-ceans, and also fish and spawn have already been explained: that is that trout preoccupied with feeding on these organisms are not easily taken by conventional fly fishing. It may be interesting to note that stream " B " is the only one with a significant head of grayling, but that stream " A " also carries a selection of coarse fish, none of whose spawn is apparent.

The ratings for terrestrial animals are *not* distorted, which brings me to the graph, shown as Table 3, demonstrating the rela-tive percentage of terrestrial creatures found in trout stomach contents on all three waters throughout the trout season. The June dip is almost certainly attributable to the mayfly contribution of stream " A ", but the July/August peak sheds some doubt on the validity of the " absence of fly " excuse for the falling off of sport in those months, at any rate as far as these waters are con-cerned!

While proffering these tables as interesting information, I do not propose to draw any specific conclusions—indeed I do not think that it is possible to do so: as they stand they could be

TABLE 3

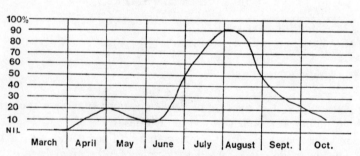

PROPORTION OF TERRESTRIAL INSECTS IN TROUT STOMACHS.

(Aquatic organisms in reverse proportions).

made to endorse some conclusions which I have already presented and at the same time to contradict others. If they were broken down into component months more accurate conclusions could probably be drawn, but perhaps at the cost of confusing many of my readers.

However, from Dr. Lloyd's final group of figures I *do* propose to point up a (possibly tendentious) conclusion, although not necessarily for any waters other than stream " B ", from which they are taken. They may also be regarded as rather inconclusive since they cover only the months of July, August and September of one season: if they could have included some of the grayling taken by me in June, for example, the shrimp figure for grayling would overshadow all others. The figures detail in percentages the respective stomach contents of trout and grayling killed over the same period.

TABLE 4

		Grayling %	Trout %
Simulium (reed smuts)	Flies	–	16
	Larvae	3	–
Stoneflies	Flies	3	36
	Larvae	67	–
Caddis (sedge)	Flies	–	6
	Larvae	5	3
Ephemeropterans	Duns/spinners	–	1
	Nymphs	17	1
Limpets		1	–
Shrimps		3	–
Terrestrial insects, etc.		4	37

COMPARISON OF STOMACH CONTENTS OF TROUT AND GRAYLING (July to September).

This table seems to indicate a text-book example of a " Jack Spratt " syndrome; at least it would appear to demonstrate, irrespective of what may happen, or be alleged to happen, elsewhere, that on this water during these months neither species of fish is taking food out of the other's mouth!

POSTSCRIPT

WHEN FIRST I sat down to write this book, rather more than a year ago, I began by speculating on why I was doing so and why so many others do so. I am no nearer to that answer even now, but one thing I have discovered is a reason why I would like to write another if I have it in me, and perhaps the reason why others also, having written one book go on to write a second, and so on. It is that in the writing of it I have learned so much more than I knew previously! If this book can increase a reader's knowledge by as much as it has increased mine, then I feel that it will all have been well worthwhile. If this sounds paradoxical, let me try to explain.

Throughout one's fishing life one picks up numerous " pre-packed " pieces of advice: call them axioms or aphorisms or dogmas or just plain wrinkles, what they amount to are bits of other people's knowledge which by reading or word-of-mouth one has absorbed into the sum of one's own fishing information, un-consciously to be turned up at the appropriate time when they appear to be appropriate to the current situation. They are very essential to the fabric of an individual's fishing knowledge because each is a small short cut in the road to accomplished angling—without them few fishermen could achieve competence in a normal lifetime, for too much time would be expended in feeling a way by trial and error. Nevertheless each fragment of information needs testing by each angler, for while it may have been entirely valid in the circumstances in which it originated, the circum-stances in which one resurrects it may not be the same—the water may not be the same, nor the weather, nor the time of year, nor the temperature nor the barometer, nor countless other factors in-cluding the angler himself.

Now this book (like all others about fishing) is filled with such bits of information, some explicit, some implicit; some consciously emphasised, others taken for granted; a few based on my own discovery but owing their origin to other sources, the majority from my own collection of other men's experience.

It occurred to me that it would be quite wrong consciously to pass on any information which I had not personally tested and satisfied myself that it was valid in the context of the type of fishing which I was attempting to describe, and I do not mean in a purely physical sense: it was necessary to be theoretically valid. This has led me to have a continuous series of arguments with myself, the effect of which has been in some cases to modify or even to reverse a conclusion towards which I had been working. In one or two instances (I dare not say where) having written down something approaching mild dogma I have proceeded to argue the pros and cons with myself to such good effect that finally I have needed to expunge the statement and replace it with something not far from its opposite!

This is what I mean when I say that this book has taught me much, and it must be worth something to start with one satisfied customer, even if he *is* prejudiced and in a minority!

Luston, Herefordshire,
January, 1971

INDEX

of fly dressings described in the text.